LIFE IS ABUNDANT

21 Days to Manifest What You Want,
Raise Your Vibration,
And Easily Attract More Good in Your Life

SHANNON N. SMITH

Powerful You!
PUBLISHING
Sharing Wisdom ~ Shining Light

LIFE IS ABUNDANT
21 Days to Manifest What You Want, Raise Your Vibration,
And Easily Attract More Good in Your Life

Copyright © 2023

Published by: Powerful You! Inc. USA

powerfulyoupublishing.com

Library of Congress Control Number: 2023907737

Shannon N. Smith – First Edition

ISBN: 978-1-959348-14-6

First Edition May 2023

BODY MIND & SPIRIT / Inspiration & Personal Growth

Acknowledgements

Thank you…

To my mom and dad for always supporting and believing in me.

To my tribe for your support.

To my team for reminding me who I am.

Table of Contents

Introduction

Big love and gratitude to you for saying yes to yourself and your life by embarking on this 21-day journey of gratitude. You are in for a treat, my friend, for this journey encompasses so much more than twenty-one days. It is the catalyst for major shifts—a kickoff point for a happier, healthier, more balanced life. My name is Shannon and I'll be your guide. I am a healer, speaker, coach, author, lover of the human body, and a life-long learner. As you have probably guessed from the title of this book, I am also a big believer in the importance of mindset, specifically the power of gratitude.

It wasn't always like this.

I knew the word gratitude and gave it freely to things outside myself. In fact, I was so comfortable celebrating others that it never dawned on me to apply the concept to myself. Instead, I lived a life of complacency, a victim of my circumstances, and struggled to find a positive spin to the things that "didn't work out."

Sound familiar?

When was the last time you told yourself, "You are doing a good job, and despite everything you've been through you're still standing, pushing, and showing up. I'm proud of you!"?

A few years ago, I asked this of myself and was saddened by the answer. As I was doing my daily gratitude journaling I realized I wasn't celebrating myself. I was saying I was grateful for things, but it was very passive—there was no excitement behind the words. So, in 2020 I decided to challenge myself. For the first twenty-one days of June, my birthday month, I would find something in my life to be grateful for and openly celebrate. I would allow myself to reflect on my life and do an open, honest, and unapologetic exploration into everything that made me, me.

At first I struggled, but by the end of the twenty-one days, I was so proud of myself. I was able to see how far I'd come and how much I had to be grateful for. I also started to get really excited for my future. I started to see everything that was working in my favor and ended up doing some deep healing as well.

As a result of this challenge, I've come to appreciate the true meaning of gratitude and to make it a central part of my life. With this shift, I've mended relationships, attracted opportunities, improved my health and peace of mind, increased my confidence, and more. I also work with my clients to help them expand their sense of gratitude so they can make life-changing shifts too. Once you get gratitude down, you can't ever go wrong.

My intention for this challenge and workbook is for you to take time for yourself daily to show appreciation and gratitude for your life—every single aspect, regardless of your current perception of the good, the bad, or the ugly. This is an invitation to explore and examine your life, falling back in love with it and yourself. To gain a new perspective on who you are and why.

For the next twenty-one days, we will explore a number of topics, some expected and some not, but stick with me and I promise you will gain something from it. Each day there are exercises and questions to spark and support your exploration, healing, and growth. Each day is different, which means some exercises will require a little more time and effort to complete. Don't get discouraged, though, you can do this! I believe in you. I've found it helpful to dedicate a specific time each day for my gratitude practice, which may also be helpful for you. Find a good time and settle in with your favorite pen and a comfy chair—perhaps even light a candle to set the mood for this work. Do whatever feels good for you, my friend.

There is space here in the book to write your answers for each exercise, but if you have a separate journal that may be helpful to write down additional thoughts and feelings that come up as you reflect on the topics and move through your day.

I can't wait to see what you uncover in your journey! Shall we begin?

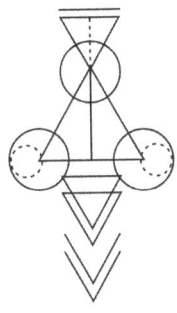

DAY 1

Measure me, baby!

*"Between stimulus and response there is space.
In that space is our power to choose our response.
In our response lies our growth and our freedom." ~ Viktor E. Frankl*

Change is inevitable and when it happens, we get to grow. It just depends on the way you look at it, right? To go through the next layer of becoming whoever and whatever we are in this life, we have to go through stages of growth *and* see them as gifts, even though sometimes it can be painful. Sometimes it seems like we can never get ahead because of the constant change, but we are growing through that change, nonetheless.

This step has two parts. It is an invitation to reflect and appreciate, and it is also an opportunity to deliberately look at our growth throughout our lives.

- The past – What can we reflect on and see differently because we learned and grew?
- The present – What can we see and appreciate because we are on this journey?
- The future – What can we look forward to and get excited about?

That's what I've done each time I embarked on a challenge like this, and I've learned more about myself, increased appreciation for my journey, about the people around me, and about life overall. I've grown.

This can feel like a roller coaster—some years are really heavy, and others are not. When we look back, however, we can often see that it's been great. It's been beautiful, and we have grown. That's why I give gratitude for growth, for the people on my path who push me to grow (more than I want to some days), and even for the discomfort, so I can actually find comfort in it. What I mean by that is not having all the answers, not controlling every aspect, but simply allowing yourself to breathe and go with the flow and be okay with not having it together all the time.

For me, that has taken growth. I have to celebrate myself for it because I've always been the person who had it together, had answers, and looked out for other people. A lot of women are in that position, whether it's by choice or the role that they step into by default. Over the last couple of years, I've been consciously trying to step *out* of that and be more in flow. It's been a process, but a good one. Day to day, moment to moment, I've been able to find more of what feels good. What doesn't feel good? Should I do this right now, or something else? Am I doing this out of obligation, or because it will contribute to my goals? All of those things.

I give gratitude to the people who push me, but also to myself for putting in the work to grow, step up, do and be more. This allows me to explore more of who I am, and be more to the people who need me to show up on a daily basis. So, I invite you to look at your journey today and see where you can celebrate your own growth.

Can you see it? If you're having a hard time getting started, here are a few examples.

You have grown if you:

- Remained calm in a situation that previously would have sparked your temper
- Said no to ice cream when normally you would have said yes
- Established and held a boundary with someone when you used to cave in

- Opted for self-care instead of pushing through your to-do list

All of these things are growth! It can look however you want, but it's time to get in celebration mode and start seeing how far we've come and how much we have to be grateful for.

Today's Exploration

Exercise

In the table below you are going to celebrate your growth in ten areas. In each space, write out your agreement or disagreement with the statement from five years ago and now. How would you have responded then and how do you respond now? Your goal is to document and see that you've grown, even a little, in all or most areas.

Growth Area	5 years ago	Now
Not having to control everything and being more in flow		
Being comfortable making decisions		
Using my voice and standing up for myself		
Supporting others in new and different ways		

Growth Area	5 years ago	Now
Feeling comfortable in my skin		
Judging myself and others		
Showing up in new and different ways		
Doing things even when I'm feeling scared		
My ability to forgive myself and others		
My ability to follow my heart and intuition		

Daily Clearing

❋ I'm grateful for the growth I've experienced in my life.

❋ I release anywhere I've judged myself for not being in a certain place or not having reached a specific level of growth.

❋ I release the need to compete or compare my growth with others, for my journey is mine and mine alone.

❋ I release any expectations or projections from others about how and at what pace I grow.

❋ I forgive myself and others who have placed judgments and expectations about how growth looks or feels.

Additional Thoughts

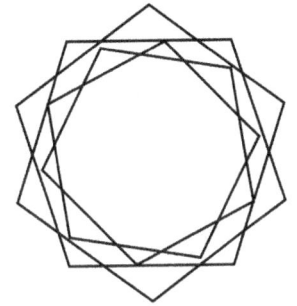

Day 2

Set Yourself Free

"Forgiveness does not change the past,
but it does enlarge the future."
~ Paul Boose

Forgiveness isn't likely something you'd expect to celebrate, and this is exactly why we need to tackle it—so you can understand and experience the impact it has on our daily lives. I used to think forgiveness was pointless. I was the person who held onto a grudge until death. The reason didn't matter—if I felt hurt or wronged in some way (even by someone I cared for deeply) it was on! I didn't realize how much that was impacting me though because my ego told me it was about the other person. Little did I know I was carrying the burden and it very much was affecting me, my well-being, and my ability to think clearly. Now I understand how it can help us release the past, appreciate the present, and help propel us into our future.

What is forgiveness, really? It is essentially a release of a burden you've been carrying. I have experienced the truth of this. The more forgiveness I've done, the more helpful it's been, the more layers I shed, and the more expansive I feel.

Forgiveness is not excusing another's bad behavior. You may have heard a saying to the effect of, "Forgive, not for the other person, but for yourself." I know I physically felt heavier because I let other people's mess influence my life. I now know that is not the way to operate. All the little things from high school and college; the relationships that didn't work out; the friends who did you wrong or the so-and-sos who tried to take advantage of you...it's just not worth holding on to. And today is the day we dig into that and begin to look at situations as an observer.

Looking at a situation as the observer means removing emotion and seeing facts. It's using compassion and saying, "There might be some circumstances beyond my control or understanding, but I may not need to understand them and that's okay. There could be so many different things at play here and it does not have to impact the way that I interact with this person or others. I get to choose the way I carry myself and whether I let this hold me back."

One thing I learned over the last three or so years was that people have more going on than they show. We only receive their response, which could have been caused by something at home, a bad day, a hurtful comment, or anything else. Their response isn't who they are or how they feel about you, it is simply a reaction or projection.

Being able to see that there is something behind what the person is bringing forward has helped me understand and realize that we're all going through things—and that people might not even mean what they're saying. They may not understand the impact, which requires a level of grace from us and, ultimately, the ability to forgive. Again, this is not for them, but for you. Let them carry the drama, burdens, and projections. You don't have time for that! It's getting in the way of your magic and your ability to see it. Forgive them for the way they've made you feel as a result of their actions (whether it is intentional or not) and let it go.

Having that awareness has been monumental for me because I blamed people for things for many years. I didn't see their lack of awareness or tools, just their response and my feelings. Now I can look back on many situations and see that the person's reaction had nothing to do with me. Have you ever done that?

It's also made me more aware of how I react to others. I think we could be a lot happier and more productive if we thought about what we're carrying around (e.g. anger, shame, judgment, and frustration) and used forgiveness to release those burdens. It's time to give ourselves permission to be free. When we take things personally, we must ask if there's another place that reaction can be directed or if it's the appropriate response.

I gave myself permission to be hurt but it didn't mean that I had to carry others' supposed shortcomings within me. And over time I've learned to let my hurt be the invitation for questions that allow healing. I've done that exercise countless times, but I do it energetically with people and it is extremely powerful. I can forgive because I see my part in it and I see their part in it. I might not understand it all, but I can see both sides and I don't fault them. There's nothing to blame or fix; I just release and move on.

This was key for my healing process because I was able to sift through life situations and apply this. It helped me discern what was my responsibility to take care of and what was someone else's. I also learned to forgive myself, which was equally important, and to take ownership of my stuff without blame. Whoa, the relief that comes with that! It feels good to know that we don't have to deal with things that are not ours. We've all heard stories of a horrific tragedy where a parent loses their child or another loved one and they say they will forgive the aggressor. It wasn't until I started this work that I finally understood how they could do that—and why. When we release someone else's burden, we give ourselves the space to do our own work and open up possibilities in our lives.

So, today we celebrate forgiveness for the relief and freedom it brings. It's time to make space for more good. There is valuable space being taken up—energetically, physically, and emotionally—by petty grudges and perceived wrongdoings. This also allows you to reclaim your power. The simple act of letting it go and letting it be has improved all aspects of my life. Once I flipped that switch, my focus shifted and I began to feel better; I felt empowered. I want that for you too.

I celebrate forgiveness because it allows for clarity, and with clarity, you expedite progress and growth. Without forgiveness there is resistance, which invites frustration, blockages, and delays in our lives. Think about that for a minute. What else could be possible if you simply let those things go? What could life be like? What could you create? Working on forgiveness has helped me manifest money, opportunities, connections to people, improved health, growth, clarity, and so much more!

Now, enough talk about forgiveness—let's get to the meat of it!

The most frequent exercise I do is based on a Hawaiian exercise called Ho'o pono pono. It is simple: you get quiet and take a few minutes to visualize who you want to forgive. It could be one person or it could be a group, but the idea is you imagine yourself in a theater where there is a stage and seats for an audience. Here are the steps:

1. Stand on the stage, with your person/people sitting in the audience.
2. Invite the person to the stage and visualize that person walking onto the stage, facing you.
3. Talk to the person and say, "I see you. I accept you. I forgive you. I love you. Thank you." You are allowing yourself to see and accept them for who/what they are and what they may have done. You are offering forgiveness to them because of this acceptance. Then you extend love and gratitude for the experience.
4. Ask the person to reciprocate, stating the same back to you.
5. Offer a word of forgiveness to yourself to release any remaining energy.
6. Offer a hug and ask for both of you to be restored physically and energetically. Depending on the person it could be a handshake, but I've found some form of physical acknowledgment is helpful.
7. The person returns to the audience, walks off the stage, or simply disappears when you feel you're done. And that's it! That's the process.

Do this for each person you want to forgive. It may seem like a lot of steps, but once you get the hang of it, you'll move through pretty quickly.

This isn't a one-and-done type of exercise, however. The first time I did this I felt immense relief, but realized that once I shifted energetically, I would have another angle or layer pop up, so I could do the exercise from a new perspective and experience more benefits. You may find this for yourself. And another key I've found is the "thank you" part. Since we are doing this as a way to increase the gratitude in our lives, being willing to acknowledge the lessons and positive aspects of a person or situation helps with the process. When we're able to come from a place of gratitude, we neutralize the energy around a situation and that's where the fun begins!

Today's Exploration

Questions

1. What is your relationship with forgiveness?

_____

_____

_____

_____

2. What role has it played in your life? Have you experienced any benefits from it?

_____

_____

_____

_____

3. Have you noticed any impacts from this relationship (positive or negative)?

_____

_____

_____

_____

4. Where do your beliefs about forgiveness come from?

_____

_____

_____

_____

Exercise

In each of the spaces below, write the name of a person or situation you're ready to forgive. Then, for each person or situation, say, "I see you. I accept you. I forgive you. I love you. Thank you." Don't forget to give yourself permission to experience any feelings or emotions that come out in this process. All of it is relevant and part of your process. Also, feel free to use additional paper if needed.

1. _____

2. _____

3. _____

4. _____

5. _____

6. _____

7. _____

8. _____

9. _____

10. _____

11. _____

12. _____

13. _____

14. _____

15. _____

16. _____

17. _____

18. _____

19. _____

20. _____

Daily Clearing

❋   It is safe for me to forgive others.

❋   It is safe for me to experience the relief of forgiveness.

❋   Anywhere I've believed that I am wrong for completing the process of forgiveness, I release myself from these beliefs and anyone who has imparted them to me.

❋   It is safe for me to forgive myself and acknowledge that I always do my best.

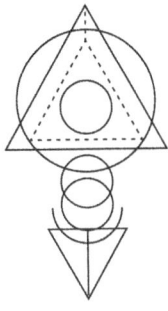

Day 3

Because I Care

"Talk to yourself like you would to someone you love."
~ Brené Brown

Today we are talking about self-care. I used to think about this topic and associate it with getting a massage or taking a relaxing bath. Over time, however, my definition has evolved significantly—from not really paying attention to it to prioritizing it and making it a regular occurrence. Self-care won't necessarily look the same for you as it does for me. It's different for all of us and changes throughout our lives. That's something that I had to learn.

We can all benefit from expanding our idea of self-care. Yes, it can be a massage or bath, but it can also be cooking yourself a nice meal, going for a walk, cleaning, and turning on your favorite music and dancing it out. It could even mean having that piece of cake because that's what feels good, not because you're emotionally eating, not because you're trying to get comfort from the food and avoid dealing with something, but because it simply tastes delicious!

I wish I knew this years ago and was willing to invite it into my life the way I do now. I've always loved massages and being outside and things like that. I've never been a bath person, though, so I thought, *Oh well, I don't do self-care because I don't do those things that most people say 'self-care' is.* I like to work out; I like to relax and watch movies; I like to sleep—all of which, I learned, are acts of self-care! Essentially, self-care is anything that nourishes our mental health, physical health, emotional health, spiritual health, and psychological health—and it is so important.

Our lives are filled with many different kinds of stressors, so finding balance and calm allows us to connect to our bodies, intuition, loved ones, and more. That's where self-care comes in. I used to be the person that said, "I'll sleep when I'm dead." Yes, those words came out of my mouth, most often in college because I didn't want to miss out on anything. There are thousands of studies on sleep deprivation that tell you the harm that we do to ourselves when we don't sleep. But this is where I was. Can you relate?

Operating in that mindset took its toll on all aspects of my life. Learning that it doesn't always have to be essential oils and baths was a relief for me—though of course, those things are great if that's what floats your boat. Regardless of how it looks, you deserve self-care and get to do it any way you want. It helps you and everyone around you when you prioritize it. My top self-care is floating (in the saltwater float tank), massage, and dancing. Sometimes it's sleep, cooking food, or watching a cool movie. It fluctuates. You may also fluctuate and not realize it. Sometimes I clean when I feel stuck and need to make space to think. What's important is my ability to see the differences, be aware of what I need, and then make a point to get it into my life so I can feel better. So, I prioritize self-care and honor how it looks on a day-to-day basis because that allows more flow in my life.

I've learned I always feel better when I'm honoring what my body needs, what my systems need, and what my environment is asking of me. It's a priority in my health regimen. Five years ago, I wouldn't have said that, but after all I've learned about the body—how our environment impacts us, how our bodies respond to the things we consume, and how the people around us affect our energy—I know how critical it is.

Getting to this space was major growth. The more I've been able to do this and set boundaries (another form of self-care) to create the environment that feels best for me, the better I feel and the more I'm able to serve. Do you know what self-care looks like for you? Do you honor your need for self-care, or is that on the back burner because of other obligations—your own or someone else's? That's what we're digging into today, so get ready!

Today's Exploration

Questions

1. How has your relationship with self-care been up to this point?

_____

_____

_____

_____

2. List 5 of your favorite self-care practices.

_____

_____

_____

_____

3. Now, narrow it down to your favorite. Can you do it today or this week? Write down when/where you will do it so you don't forget.

_____

_____

_____

_____

4. How can you make this a regular occurrence for yourself and your schedule? You may want to pay attention to any "reasons" you think this can't happen and write them down.

_____

_____

_____

_____

Daily Clearing

❋   I am worthy of taking care of myself in ways that feel good to me.

❋   I am free to define self-care any way I want that feels good to me.

❋   Anywhere I've taken on the ideas of someone else related to self-care, I release them now.

❋   I forgive myself for not prioritizing myself and my self-care before now.

❋   I am grateful for all of the ways I have to take care of myself.

Additional Thoughts

Day 4

Reminders of Who I Am

*"The cosmos is within us. We are made of star-stuff.
We are a way for the universe to know itself."
~ Carl Sagan*

Have you ever had an experience where you felt like you were in the zone? Like you brought everything you had to a situation and simply delivered or executed effortlessly? It felt good; everyone involved felt good, and it all just worked out. I love those moments. We all have at least one where we had an amazing meeting or conversation. Or we hit the winning shot in the game. Or we closed a deal and got a new client. That feeling is so many things wrapped into one that it can be hard to express in words. But one thing is clear: you brought all of who you are.

I think back to a time when I did that. It was teaching my first energy healing certification class. I was so nervous leading up to it and even as the class started, but by the end, we all felt amazing, relaxed, and healed. It was such a magical space to be in. I remember walking outside to decompress but also to bask in my accomplishment because I was relieved and proud of what I had just done. It was such a good day!

This was a reminder of who I am. What I am referring to here is being in the teaching space or sharing my experience and knowledge with others so they can do more in their lives and pass it on. It felt really good to be in the position of teacher and mentor again—and learning from the class attendees as well. Have you heard of the concept of "entangled hierarchy"? It's when there is no higher or lower than based on title or experience. No one is put on a pedestal because they are facilitating, rather it's an exchange of information and energy—a beautiful space where everyone is a teacher, everyone is a learner. That's how it should be! I often ask what life would be like if we could create more spaces like that, but that is another topic for another day. Our class was amazing and everyone felt great after.

I was grateful for the reminder that this was something I could do because I enjoy it. This particular opportunity was really important because I was in a rebuilding phase and recreating my life. What am I doing? Who do I want to be? Who do I want to show up as? What's right? What's wrong? What feels good and doesn't?—these were all questions I was asking myself at the time. I was evaluating patterns and habits to keep and release. I was ready to shift and everything was on the table, but you know what? I needed something to show me I was on the right track. I needed a little boost.

That class was my reminder of my capacity to do the things I desire, and that it would be beneficial to do more things like it. That I enjoy this type of activity and feel good doing it, not only for myself but for those engaging me. It lights me up when I'm able to help others see more possibilities for themselves and that was the space I helped to create that day. In my book, that's always a win-win situation.

Sometimes it's easy to get down on ourselves and forget that we are capable of more than our daily routine. We are capable of helping others if we want. We are capable of creating magic and being that magic for ourselves and others. I think we periodically need reminders that we're okay. That we're doing good, that it's possible to feel good if we aren't currently, or, if we are feeling good, we can feel even better. Sometimes we're just in a rut and we question things. We have fear or uncertainty and talk ourselves out of our destiny.

Today is your reminder of who you are and the power that lies within. You are doing good. You can feel good. You can contribute. You can be the healer. You can be the teacher. You can be the lover. You can be the catalyst. And don't worry, you aren't alone—I need these reminders periodically too. It's nice to collect experiences as proof of your capabilities—those when you allowed yourself to step into all of you and show up fully as that.

So that is what we're celebrating today—those opportunities to show up as all of who you are. Today, you get to dive into your magic!

Today's Exploration

Questions

1. What past reminders have you received of who you really are? List 3.

_____

_____

_____

_____

2. How did those experiences make you feel? List 3 words.

_____

_____

_____

_____

3. What reminders have you had today of who you truly are and who/what you were meant to be in this world?

_____

_____

_____

_____

4. What feelings come up when you think about who you really are? List 5 things.

_____

_____

_____

_____

5. What actions/activities do you do to make you feel this way?

_____

_____

_____

_____

6. How can you get more of that in your day today? What about your week?

_____

_____

_____

_____

7. What words would you use to describe you in all of your magic?

_____

_____

_____

_____

8. What is something that has gotten in the way of you showing up as all of who you are?

_____

_____

_____

_____

9. What is one thing you can do now to rewrite your story about that?

_____

_____

_____

_____

Daily Clearing

❋   It is safe for me to embrace, embody, and experience my life as all that I am.

❋   I release any and all limiting thoughts and behaviors preventing me from showing up as all that I am in each moment.

❋   I release any and all judgments from myself or others of where I've shown up as all that I am and it was taken the wrong way.

❋   I am grateful for all the reminders I have in my life about everything I offer to the world and how I provide value for simply being me.

❋   I set an example for others when I am willing to find ways to show up as all of me.

Additional Thoughts

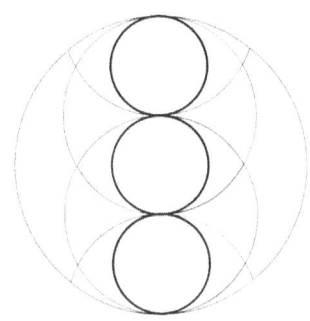

Day 5

Can You See What I See?

"Your perspective will either become your prison or your passport."
~ Steven Furtick

Today we are talking about perspective. Usually when I hear this word I think about all of our experiences, the amalgamation of those we've had, and how it shapes how we view and contribute to the world. How our ideas, dreams, and solutions come to be and how they differ from those around us. One time I won a free session with a coach I had just met. Their area of expertise intrigued me, so despite some hesitation I accepted. During the session I was able to address and release something I hadn't been able to access on my own and ended up being extremely grateful for the experience.

It really made me think about the different perspectives we bring to the work we do, particularly in coaching or energy work, but in any career or industry. The tools, modalities, certifications, and degrees that we obtain are often what people seek and use as the way to determine our fit to work together. For most of my life I talked about perspective through the lens of:

- Traveling the world and experiencing different cultures, foods, and landscapes
- Whether you have siblings or are an only child like me
- Growing up in a military family

- Working in a field different from your degree or training
- Whether you grew up in a two-parent or single-parent household
- Experiencing a medical condition or disability and having limited capacity

All of these things influence how we think, live, interact with others, and move through our day. They shape our belief system and what we think is possible for our lives. I know they impact me when I walk out the door each day, and because of this it never ceases to amaze me how similar we all are, as well as our desires for ourselves and our families. On the flip side, our different perspectives can keep us apart, preventing progress, love, and understanding. It depends on how you look at it.

The most pivotal shift in my perspective, and something that challenged me, was my health. After receiving a diagnosis and managing it I had convinced myself I was healthy. Also, despite horrible hormonal imbalances, I learned to deal with my body and still had this perspective. Then, one day, I said yes to a hypnosis session. This was very new to me at the time, but I was curious and open to the experience. Shortly after, I experienced positive body changes that led to the realization that my perspective on health had been inaccurate.

One thing I've always valued is my diverse perspective. In my consulting career, my background helped me present new and different ideas and solutions to my clients so they could transform their organizations. I once received praise for always being ready in meetings. It was because I could spin a topic or an issue ten different ways, which helped me understand different angles, be prepared for questions, and be ready to provide guidance. If you imagine a Rubik's Cube and looking at the different sides of it—that's how I treated my work back then. I also do so in my coaching/healing practice now. Being able to do that comes from exposure, experience, and being observant—it's the culmination of everything I am. When we notice something like color preferences (because a client is color blind), formatting quirks (I had a superior who only liked round bullets), and word preferences, demonstrating empathy and a desire to understand "others" perspectives as something to learn from rather than a threat, it opens up new possibilities. Answers. Growth. Connection.

We all have different strengths with different gifts that we bring to the table and that's valuable. This is why all eight billion of us are needed on this planet. It means there is massive potential for anything we want. What would happen if we each gave ourselves permission to see this in ourselves? What would happen if we allowed ourselves to let our light shine through and shared it with others? When we shut ourselves down or let others do it for us, we stay small and our magic can't be seen. When we think we're in a competition with someone else and let that dictate our lives, we lose out on experiencing everything we're meant to.

So, today we celebrate perspective—that amazing and unique perspective only you have and no one else can duplicate. We're celebrating the awareness of this and the ability to fully embrace it, because we are worth it. It's so easy to find something wrong with us or something to fix, but there's no room for that today.

Today's Exploration

Questions

1. What are five unique things about you that you're proud of?

_____

_____

_____

_____

2. What characteristics make up who you are?

_____

_____

_____

_____

3. Are you comfortable claiming your unique perspective? Why or why not? Where does this belief come from?

_____

_____

_____

_____

4. What in your experience contributes to your unique perspective?

_____

_____

_____

_____

5. What about your perspective are you proud of?

_____

_____

_____

_____

6. How does your perspective differentiate you and add value to others?

_____

_____

_____

_____

7. How can you begin to help others more using your perspective?

_____

_____

_____

_____

8. What is one way you can use your unique experience and perspective to help someone or contribute in a way that only you can do?

_____

_____

_____

_____

Daily Clearing

✳ I am grateful for and celebrate all of the things that make me uniquely me.

✳ I release any judgments I have of myself, or that others have had about me, regarding my unique experience.

✳ I forgive myself for not being able to see the beauty in my unique experience.

✳ I'm grateful to have exposure to others who are different from me and contribute to me with their unique experiences.

✳ I am beautifully, powerfully, magically, and unapologetically unique and valuable just for being me.

✳ I choose to release anywhere that I've decided that being me is "too much" or "too little" or that my uniqueness isn't worth showing.

Additional Thoughts

Day 6

Believing is Seeing

"I believe in intuitions and inspirations.
I sometimes feel that I am right. I do not know that I am."
~ Albert Einstein

We call it by many names: "trusting our gut"; "listening to your heart"; "Divine guidance." I call it intuition. It's something we're born with, can use at any time, and develop to make it stronger. That's where we're going today because I'm extremely grateful for mine and I'd like you to see where yours has been helpful along the way—whether you knew it at the time or not.

Something I've always been good at is hearing from my intuition. For as long as I can remember, I've received messages and guidance to help me along my journey. The problem is, I didn't listen to it for years. (FYI: there is a big difference between hearing and listening.) I didn't know where it was coming from and because I had expectations about how intuition worked, I dismissed it.

I would know something felt good or bad but rarely acted on that feeling because I was so used to listening to things outside of myself. When my gut feeling was different from what people I loved and respected said I went with them because that's what we're taught to do. I wasn't one to ruffle feathers or go against the grain much, so following was easy. Little did I know I was silencing and negating a very powerful tool.

Because some of the things my intuition wanted me to do early on were scary and seemed outlandish, I didn't do them. I was in my logical brain and didn't have the capacity to feel things out. It was weird to have a feeling about something without having tangible evidence of the potential outcome. If something felt off, I wanted proof of what "off" meant so I could believe it and vice versa. Seeing was believing.

What I've learned is that it doesn't work like that. Intuition and ego go hand in hand, they're just opposites kind of like the proverbial angel and devil on our shoulders. The angel is our intuition saying to do the things that feel good and light us up. Sometimes it's a little scary, but the voice is comforting so it's a little easier to hear it and possibly listen. It's like the friend who wants the very best for us. The devil tells us that it's wrong and don't do it because there's fear, others don't do it, which equates to a threat. It doesn't want us to be seen, heard, or grow, so it's better to be safe. If we aren't taught to see the difference, life can be difficult.

There have also been several times when I had a gut feeling and listened to it. One I'll never forget was during finals week in college. I needed to get on campus to take my test and was almost running late. However, something told me to wait. *I thought, No, this can't be right. I need to go now*, but for some reason, I listened. Eventually, I did leave and soon found myself on the main road halfway to campus. As I approached a light, intending to turn right, another car sped past me, just having gone through the turn, followed by a cop car going the wrong direction in traffic. Had I not delayed, I would've been hit head-on. Can you believe that?!

What about when you had a gut feeling and *didn't* follow it? I remember scanning through several hotels online while booking a trip. One caught my eye, and though it looked nice my gut said no. I didn't book it then but ended up doing so when I had to go back through that city. Despite the earlier "no" I wanted to check it out. I ended up getting food poisoning at breakfast and was extremely sick on my way to another city.

So how do we get more consistent with *hearing* our intuition and *actually listening* to what it says? For me it's taken practice, and releasing expectations. Another key is consulting it when making decisions. As I said earlier, I listened to others and negated my intuition often, so I rarely knew if a decision was good for me until it was too late.

These days, I consult my intuition *first*. If I get a gut feeling I pause to listen and understand what it's saying, then act. I follow my feelings and trust that they are leading me in the right direction. I turn it into a game and ask for guidance on everything—exercise, food, rest, tasks, and opportunities. If my gut response feels shaky, I ask others, then compare the feelings and act only when I feel like there's enough information. Life has gotten sweeter in the process. There's been more flow, healing, and expansion because I'm more connected to my internal guidance. I'm extremely grateful for this tool because the possibilities are now endless.

Today's Exploration

Questions

1. When was the last time you had a gut feeling and trusted it? What happened?

_____

_____

_____

_____

2. Have you ever had a gut feeling and not trusted it? What happened?

_____

_____

_____

_____

3. Is it normal for you to trust your intuition or gut feeling? Why or why not?

_____

_____

_____

_____

4. Are there people around you who follow their gut? What does that look like?

_____

_____

_____

_____

5. What is something you can do to increase your trust in your intuition?

_____

_____

_____

_____

Exercise

Now, it's your turn to connect to your intuition. You've seen some of my examples, so now you get to see what yours wants you to know about something in your life. Pick a topic or situation you are currently dealing with. Tune into your gut, heart, intuition now...what does it tell you about what to do?

_____

_____

_____

_____

Daily Clearing

❋   I am connected to all layers of me and all of the information accessible to me.

❋   I trust my intuition and where it guides me.

❋   I release anywhere I've blocked my ability to hear my internal guidance.

❋   I release anywhere I've been harmed for using my internal guidance.

❋   I release any expectations of what I, or others, think it looks or feels like to use, follow, and trust my intuition.

❋   I release from my body any projections or judgments from myself or others about what it means to trust and follow my intuition.

Additional Thoughts

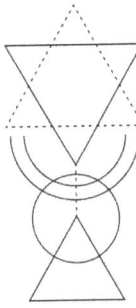

Day 7

Making Lemonade From Lemons

"The greater the contrast, the greater the potential.
Great energy only comes from a correspondingly great tension of opposites."
~Carl Jung

We've all gone through unpleasant or painful things that, for the life of us, we couldn't understand. Why did this happen and, more specifically, why did it have to happen to us?! Abraham-Hicks refers to these experiences as "contrast." I believe there are many reasons we deal with contrast, but mostly it's because there's something we need to learn or an experience we need to gain before we get to our next level.

On Day 19 there is a story about a client yelling at me at work. I go back to that story almost twenty years later because it clearly demonstrates how I needed that experience to get to the next level of my career. I have countless stories of contrast in a professional environment and even though they totally sucked at the time, I became an amazing consultant and mentor as a result of them. And I've been able to translate these experiences to all areas of my life, so it's a total win!

The autoimmune diagnosis I received is another thing I'd consider contrast. I physically couldn't do a lot of the things I was used to doing. It caused me to adapt every aspect of my life whether I was ready to accept what was going on or not. While in the thick of it, I resented so many things because I thought I was being punished for something. But eventually, I was able to see that all the changes I made—in all aspects of my life—were actually necessary for me to get here with you. The gifts, expansion, discovery, and so much more that have come from it are priceless. But I had to go through the contrast, sort through the muck, learn the lessons, and change to get to the other side.

I can guarantee you that this book you're holding in your hands would not exist if I didn't go through that experience. It's been difficult, but so much good has come from it for me and others.

Contrast has taught me that we don't always get our way and that's okay. When we experience contrast it means we're working through something to get to a better place. They say one door closes and another opens, right? That's what we're talking about. There is a greater plan at play if we're willing to walk through every experience to see what we can gain from it and then reap the benefits after. My gratitude wasn't in place either, so I couldn't appreciate it.

Can you imagine how life would be if we got everything we wanted right when we wanted it? Do you think that would be good or bad? I can honestly say that I'm glad I didn't get some things when I wanted them years ago. I wasn't ready, I was thinking too small, my mindset wasn't in the right place, nor was my environment. So how can you flip your approach to surrendering to where you are and finding the good, lessons, and opportunities for growth you'll need at the next level?

Let's talk quickly about triggers, too, because they fit nicely here. For our purposes, I'm defining a trigger as something that sparks an emotional response—positive or negative. This is when we are going about our day and all of a sudden we're upset or nervous or sad. Another person could be involved or it could be a situation. Either way, a resonance has been activated.

Before beginning energy work I thought of triggers as bad things and judged myself, and others, for the response. I think this is another thing we're not taught to adequately work through so when I started diving into this work, it was really eye-opening. When we're triggered it means there is room to grow. It means there is something that has struck a chord and we have the opportunity to address it.

It's important, just like emotions, to understand the trigger and why you're reacting in a certain way. What is the lesson and how can you change? So, again, we're brought back to...questions. Yes! I love questions and this is why. We get to investigate where the triggers come from and why we're responding the way we do. We can also choose to respond differently in the future.

The first time I approached someone who triggered me was terrifying. Yet I also understood why it was important to work through it. These conversations aren't about blaming or judging the other person, it's all about us. So even though this first conversation was hard it was so beneficial. I felt relieved and the other person found some things to heal themselves.

All of this work has helped me tremendously to understand myself and how I interact with others. I'm extremely grateful for the learning and opportunity it brings, and you too will see how helpful it can be (if you don't already do this).

Today's Exploration

Exercise

Today you are diving into an area of contrast in your life. This is going to be done in two stages. First, you will find proof of a time when you've overcome contrast and what you gained from the experience now that it's over. Then you are going to evaluate an area in your life where you are currently experiencing contrast and determine why you hold this belief and what you are meant to gain.

It can be a situation with a specific person or something else, but you are going to evaluate the situation to understand why you consider it to be contrast and what you think you are meant to learn/gain from the experience.

Proof

Current Situation

Daily Clearing

❋ I am grateful for the ability to understand my response to situations and for the tools to work through responses that may be holding me back.

❋ I am able to work through any situation I experience with ease and grace.

❋ I release anywhere I've decided that I don't have options to move through the situations I experience and/or I cannot use my experiences for good.

❋ I forgive myself for anywhere I've held onto a situation or person because I was afraid to move through the contrast or trigger.

❋ I claim my voice and strength to heal anywhere I'm holding blocks that prevent me from gaining clarity about my experiences.

❋ I release any and all judgments, expectations, and projections from myself or others regarding my responses to situations.

Additional Thoughts

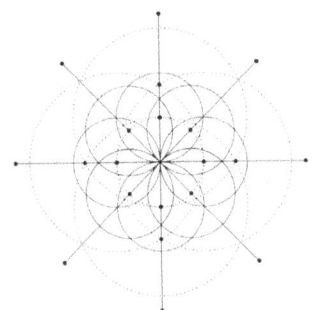

Day 8

A Neutral Resource

"Money is only a tool. It will take you wherever you wish.
But it will not replace you as the driver."
~ Ayn Rand

Today we are talking about money and how much we can be grateful for it. And, as usual, I'm going to ask you to consider a few things that may challenge your current belief about money as we frame it around gratitude. In the past, I had a not-so-nice relationship with money, which caused me to struggle for years. We're taught that it's necessary but taboo to talk about in certain circles. We're taught that it can bring lots of opportunities but are not educated on how to work with it or how it can work for us. There are lots of conflicting thoughts when it comes to money, or at least that has been my perception.

So, what's your relationship with money? Do you love or hate it? Are you neutral? One thing I've learned is that money, in and of itself, is neutral. It doesn't love or hate us, but, again, we've internalized many stories, beliefs, and conditions to the contrary. Relationships, even close ones, end over money. What do you believe to be true for you about it? Have you ever talked to your money? Have you asked how it wants to work for you or why it isn't sticking around or what you can do to have flow?

Hey, money, I love you. Come play with me!

What if money is an energy frequency and, when we connect to it on a certain level, it just appears? And what if in this connection we don't even think about the money because it becomes a non-issue? That's where gratitude comes in.

I used to be blind to the ability to do this. I thought money was something you earned and worked hard for. Possibly, I could have lots of it one day if I worked hard enough, got the right education, saved the right way, and connected with the right people. I may have a chance to get what I desired. Oh, and don't acquire any debt in the process, that was a no-no.

So, after college when I found myself in tons of debt, working and not able to pay all of my bills comfortably, I thought I just needed to work harder because I was doing "all of the right things." Not to mention the people around me, who believed in conditional relationships and thought that giving money was a sign of love and caring for them. There were expectations around me to give, just because.

I wasn't aware of my money, its frequency, and the disconnect. I wasn't aware of everything in my environment (including my mindset and beliefs) having an impact on whether my money supported me or wanted to flee. I had no respect—and definitely no gratitude—for my money and everything I got to do because of it. I was caught in a cycle of vilifying something that is inherently neutral.

I was not able to receive money easily because I was so used to giving. That was a hard one to process because I wanted money and in business you want people to pay you for services. When you're unable to receive or talk about money comfortably, can you see how that blocks you? When you're holding resentment and judgment about paying money out, can you see how that blocks you? When we look at these things and shift our perspective, we're able to experience change, positive change, with money. When we're able to appreciate what we have and everything that has come from it, more comes. We change the conversation and experience new things.

Now, let's turn to your perspective around debt. Think about it. When we are approved for credit, it means we are being deemed responsible and trustworthy. Yes, there are usually strings attached, like interest, but think about what you're able to do with the money. The access you now have to explore, create, and improve your life. What if you instead affirmed the positives around the situation?

- Yes, I am responsible and trustworthy.
- Yes, I know exactly what to do with my money and credit extended to me and I use it for good.
- Yes, I am grateful for the opportunity to have credit because I know others may not have the same opportunity as me.
- Thank you, financial institutions, for enabling me with the resources to help myself, my family, and others.

Now, I'm not saying that bad things can't happen with credit and debt. I've had some bad things happen myself, so I get it. What I am saying is there are other ways to approach money, which can be more helpful to our life.

Also, think about your bills and the services you pay for each month. What are you able to do because you have heat or water or internet service? Do you think about those things and give gratitude for the ability to have them and use them freely? I'll be honest with you—I didn't. I dreaded seeing bills come through and used to pay them at the last minute. I hated seeing the money going out, but I also loved having the things I obtained because of those services. That was another disconnect.

Here are three common beliefs about money and considerations to flip these beliefs around so they help us instead of hurt us.

- *Money doesn't grow on trees.* If you think about what money is made of, it's composed of paper and other fiber materials. Paper is made from bark, which comes from trees. So, money does in fact grow on trees! Not in a literal sense, but its components sure do.

- *It's the root of all evil.* Have you ever donated to a charity supporting your favorite cause? There's good in that, right? And it allowed someone else the opportunity to improve their life, didn't it? I don't know about you, but I'd bet that isn't "evil."

- *You have to work hard to get it.* Have you ever been given a gift card for your birthday or a holiday? Or have you ever been treated to a meal by someone? What did you have to do to get that meal? Did you have to put in a ten-hour day of hard labor, or did you simply have to be a friend to that person? Think about any times you've received a gift that has a monetary value.

One thing that opened my eyes to my relationship with money and debt was writing a letter. I picked a credit card and I wrote a letter to the company about my card and everything I'd been able to do because of it. I thanked them for trusting me and knowing that I am responsible. I thanked all the experiences I had and the knowledge gained because of the card. And, lastly, I thanked myself for being that person and knowing that I knew exactly what to do to be in flow with the card and the finances tied to it. Then I burned it. I felt so good afterward that I actually cried because I saw how much I had to appreciate. This is something you can do too if you'd like. It can be very eye-opening.

Today's Exploration

Exercise

Today we are evaluating our relationship with and beliefs around money. If there isn't enough space to complete the questions, grab your journal and let it flow! And don't deny yourself the ability to acknowledge and process any emotions that come up during this process. It can be a tricky one.

Questions

1. How is your relationship with your finances?

_____

_____

_____

_____

2. What feelings and thoughts come up for you when you think about your finances or debt?

_____

_____

_____

_____

3. Where do your beliefs about money come from? Are they beneficial for where you want to be?

_____

_____

_____

_____

4. Do you have a clear picture of your finances? Why or why not?

_____

_____

_____

_____

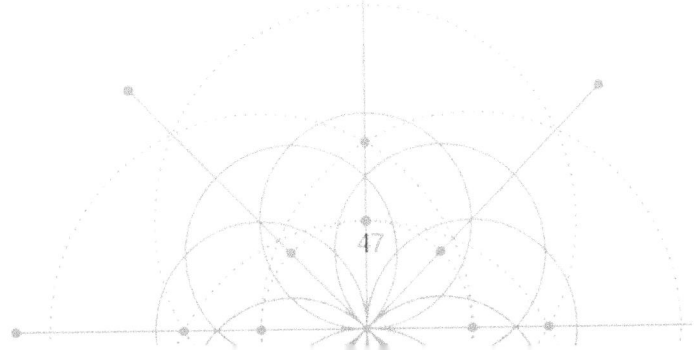

5. Pick a credit card or bank account that you use often. List 5-10 things you've been able to do because of your account/card. Then write what you're grateful for, for each thing.

_____

_____

_____

_____

6. How was the process of writing down the amazing things you've been able to do with your card/account?

_____

_____

_____

_____

Daily Clearing

* ❋   I release all fear, shame, and guilt I may be holding toward myself and my finances.
* ❋   I have an amazing relationship and partnership with money.
* ❋   I am grateful that I am surrounded by abundance and constantly in the flow of money.
* ❋   I am grateful for any and all companies that have entrusted me with the responsibility of credit.
* ❋   I love money and money loves me.
* ❋   I release everywhere I've decided that I'm not good with money and that others are entitled to more than me.
* ❋   I forgive myself for all judgments and beliefs I have that have hindered a positive relationship with money.

Additional Thoughts

Day 9

I See You, Fear!

*"And the day came when the risk to remain tight in a bud
was more painful than the risk it took to blossom."*
~ Anais Nin

I've had an interesting relationship with fear, as I think most of us do throughout our lives. When we think of fear our first response is often, "I'm afraid of something so therefore I should not do that thing." Well, my response to that is to ask, "What is driving the rationale behind the should or should not?" That's the million-dollar question, because knowing what actually dictates the rationale behind our fear in a given situation is important. This brings up the concept of how we humans are wired for survival.

When something elicits a fearful response, our bodies automatically go into that fight or flight mode, and it's like, "Oh crap. I gotta fight or get outta here or something bad is going to happen." Physically, it's a life-or-death situation—the adrenaline is pumping, the cortisol gets pumping, the blood flows to your extremities and you are ready to go. It could be that you're in the forest and a bear is about to chase you, or, more likely, that you're really mad and in an argument, feeling defenseless or you need to make a decision on something you've never done before. Your body doesn't know the difference. It just feels really scary.

Over the years my relationship with fear has evolved as I have, thank goodness. But I realize that at some point I've been afraid of everything like my life literally hung in the balance. Living, being seen, being heard, hurting someone's feelings, making the wrong decision—you name it.

But at the center of everything is the willingness or unwillingness to deal with the fear and to either see it for what it is, act through it, persevere, move through, and know that you're not actually going to be eaten by the bear. I used to let the fear paralyze me and I can't think of the number of opportunities I missed out on, the number of relationships I could've had, the things I could've avoided, had fear not gotten in the way. There are so many things that could have been possible if I had the tools that I have now to be able to see fear for what it is—simply something our brain has been programmed to deal with a certain way.

Bottom line: we need to consciously be able to differentiate between what is "safe" and what is actually unsafe. There are three profound things I always think back to when I think about my fear journey. One of them is reading *Daring Greatly* by Brené Brown, where she describes a sports arena and asks you to look at your life through this lens. Are you the person who is sitting in the stands watching others live their life on the court or are you on the court living your life? Reading that part I thought, *You know what, I'm in the stands. I am very comfortable in the stands with my seat cushion. I have my snacks and drink and I'm chilling watching everybody else live their life on the court; this proverbial "court of life."* Are you in the stands or on the court?

That section resonated with me because I'm a former athlete—on the court versus off the court was very clear in my mind. The book got me thinking about fear because I had to think about why I was in the stands. Then I had to start digging into "what am I actually afraid of?" The answer comes after the second example.

The second thing that always comes to mind when I think of fear was a mastermind coaching program I did in October 2018. We were challenged to do a Facebook Live on our personal page about one change we wanted to see in the world. The first thing that came to mind was, "Oh crap I can't do that! I can't go live. What if someone doesn't like what I have to say? People are going to see me! They're going to judge me. What if they don't like what I have to say? What if I stumble?" All the what-ifs!! To me, that was like death. Just go ahead and put me on the stake and start lighting the flames.

Have you ever had a situation like that? That's what the challenge was for me and I guarantee I experienced every single emotion and belief I've ever had about being seen, heard, liked, and accepted. I experienced them fully and wholly in my body. I waited until the last minute to do the challenge. It was a Sunday afternoon and class was on Monday. The lighting in my apartment was bad so I needed to do it before the sun went down. I finally got on and talked about wanting to see fear shift and for people to not be afraid to either step up or pursue their dreams. I talked about how fear helps us and it hurts us, but it's there for a reason and it's something that we just have to work through. My entire body shook during those three minutes.

When I closed the Live, I broke down crying for ten minutes and I had to realize that I just faced one of my biggest fears: being seen in a public arena. Wrapped in that was the potential judgment I faced after having my own thoughts and my perspectives be heard, rather than just repeating someone else's words. In the end, I got really positive feedback about the post—and I got the satisfaction of completing the challenge. I'll also say, "Don't challenge me," because I have a competitive streak and I will likely take you up on it! But it felt good to follow through on that because I learned so much about myself in that moment. And I didn't die! No bear and no stake burning!

The third thing I think of when fear comes up is a personal development program. The facilitator had a chair on the stage, which represented the fear that we had about a certain topic. They placed the chair in the middle of the stage, right in front of themselves, then posed a question like "Why are you letting fear get in the way of you moving on the other side of that chair?"

There's discussion about the reasons and excuses we have that prevent us from doing what lights us up, then we have the opportunity to think about the choices we make around fear and our particular topic. The fear is just as clear as the chair—it's never going to go away, so you have to learn to see it for what it is, talk to it, work with it, make it your friend, set it to the side, and go. For me, the visual is what solidified the message because it's so simple but clearly impeding progress between two points. When you consciously see the fear you say, "Hey, I see you. You have no power over me. I'm going to set you aside knowing that you're there but, I'm going to let you be on the side because I'm moving forward."

It can be that simple if we allow ourselves to understand what the fear is about. My own journey to having a healthy relationship with fear has been several years. Five years ago, I wouldn't have been able to talk to my fear and say, "Okay, cool. Thank you for presenting yourself. This means that I'm afraid on some level, but what's going on here? What's this about?" For so many years I saw the fear and just stopped. But now I see that chair and my power to acknowledge it and move it to the side. I allow myself to be in communion with it instead of in resistance, which gives me the space to investigate my feelings and then work through them. And ultimately, take more action in the face of fear.

Am I actually going to be eaten by the bear? No. Is someone's comment really going to ruin my life? Probably not, but it might hurt my feelings a little bit. I'm grateful for fear today because it helps me investigate imposter syndrome, excuses, and reasons for not accomplishing certain things. It's our ego trying to keep us safe, and that's okay, but there comes a time when we get to choose whether that is what runs our life or whether we're ready to take the reins. When we choose to follow what feels good, our intuition, and act even if it feels big and scary...that's when the big shifts and magic happen.

I'm grateful for fear because it's confirmation that I'm being asked to step up and do something new and different. And I can't get to my most expansive self if I keep doing the same old things, can I? Neither can you. We can see the breadcrumbs and take action a little faster because we know something better, bigger, and more amazing is on the other side. We can see that chair and say, "I know something bigger, better, greater is on the other side and I'm going for it because I run this show." Now it's your turn!

Today's Exploration

Questions

1. What fear can you be grateful for today?

_____

_____

_____

_____

2. Do you have a healthy relationship with fear and are you able to celebrate and be grateful for fear?

_____

_____

_____

_____

3. Are you living your life in the stands or on the court of your life? Why or why not?

_____

_____

_____

_____

4. Give an example of when you've looked fear in the face and acted anyway. What was the result? How did you feel about yourself?

_____

_____

_____

_____

5. Are you holding any beliefs from others about what you should feel fear about? Are these helping or hurting you?

_____

_____

_____

_____

6. Describe how your body reacts when you feel fear.

_____

_____

_____

_____

7. Develop a list of proof describing when you have conquered your fears.

_____

_____

_____

_____

8. Make a list of things that you've been fearful of that aren't really things to be afraid of.

_____

_____

_____

_____

9. What am I afraid of? What's the worst that could happen? What can I believe instead?

_____

_____

_____

_____

Daily Clearing

❋ It is safe for me to experience fear and still take action toward my goals.

❋ Having a feeling of fear means nothing wrong or bad about me.

❋ I release all past experiences where I have let fear dictate my life, thoughts, and actions.

❋ Anywhere I'm holding onto the fearful or limiting beliefs of others, I lovingly release these projections from my body, mind, and energy field.

❋ I have a healthy relationship with fear and know exactly what to do when I experience these feelings.

Additional Thoughts

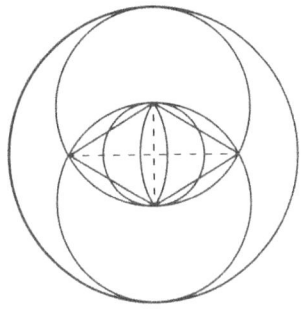

Day 10

Love Is In the Air

"Love is not an emotion, it's your very existence."
~ Rumi

Did you ever watch movies when you were young and dream of having a fairytale love? The kind where prince charming sweeps you off your feet, or where there is utter harmony, support, and love between you and your partner? You'd watch movies and television seeing people deeply in love and wonder how that happens. Or you'd see people you knew having this experience, easily feeling happy for them. I used to wonder if I'd ever have that fairytale love, or even love in any sense. For a long time, it didn't feel like that was something written in my story.

Eventually, I learned that, Number 1: Those things are scripted, and Number 2: It's an inside job. When things are scripted it plays with your mind, doesn't it? You believe that's how life really is, or at least you have a strong impression that it could be possible. You might even think that something may be wrong with you because you don't have it—the fairytale, that is. I hope I'm not the only one who used to think like this.

The concept of this being an inside job solidified when a friend said she realized why her relationships weren't adding up to this fairytale—not even close. The strong, loving relationship with someone else was missing because she didn't see love in herself. And because she didn't see love in herself, she wouldn't be able to give or receive love from another. Hearing her explain this epiphany was eye-opening. It was the first time I heard something like that and understood it. "So what you're saying is, I have to do some work on me before I can do anything with anyone else?" Yes!

Down the rabbit hole I went. Did you know that we are worthy of love, just by default? That we are born worthy and that we begin to question this when we receive the influence of other people? I didn't. We learn that there are conditions to love and we must meet these conditions to be liked, accepted, and loved. Somewhere in that we also begin to compare how we give/receive and judgment comes in. This can result in feeling like we aren't deserving of love. We compare our experience to others, live according to conditions, and form opinions about what love and life should be, based on this. And, in the process, we energetically block the very things we wish to receive.

For a long time, I didn't know I was enough so I felt I needed to give and do more to justify time with me. I gave away lots of things because I thought this is what you do when you care for people or to have friends. The recipients didn't offer anything extra special in return either, it was very lopsided. But it was me and my "not-enoughness" thinking that I needed to give above and beyond to simply be accepted. My presence wasn't enough. Somehow I developed the belief that I was deficient and needed to make up for it. I couldn't see that I was enough on my own and that I didn't need to do anything to deserve...all I had to do was *be*.

I led with my conditioning—"give in order to be accepted"— which brought me down a dangerous path and unhealthy relationship with the word love. I disassociated and became both numb and very angry. But somehow, I learned that love is in us. We are love at our core. And when we're able to see love in ourselves we're able to see it in others. And when this happens our lives can turn around. This is when my life turned around. I took accountability to release the anger and fear, allowed myself to feel, and opened up to what new perspectives I could gain about the word and concept of love.

Since learning these things, I've seen shifts in my life. My perspective and relationship with myself has shifted significantly. My relationship with others has shifted as well. I'm vibrating more at the frequency of love, appreciation, and gratitude because that's where the magic happens. I'm feeling good. Are you ready to make some magic happen?

Today's Exploration

Questions

1. What is your relationship with love?

_____

_____

_____

_____

2. Do you believe you are worthy of receiving love the same way you give it? Why or why not?

_____

_____

_____

_____

3, Where do your beliefs about love come from?

_____

_____

_____

Exercise

4. Where do you spend most of your time vibrationally? Around love and appreciation or fear and anger?

_____

_____

_____

_____

5. Describe how life is as a result and what you'd like to change.

_____

_____

_____

_____

Today we are going to bask in the love in your life! This one is simple but I want you to enjoy it. The goal is to see and know that you are surrounded by love constantly, and that is something to be grateful for!

List 5 ways you give love to others.

1. _____

2. _____

3. _____

4. _____

5. _____

List 5 ways you give love to yourself.

1. _____
2. _____
3. _____
4. _____
5. _____

List 10 ways you receive love from others.

1. _____
2. _____
3. _____
4. _____
5. _____
6. _____
7. _____
8. _____
9. _____
10. _____

Daily Clearing

* ❋ I am surrounded by love.
* ❋ I am able to see love in others as they see love in me.
* ❋ I am worthy of love and release anywhere I've believed anything different from this.
* ❋ It is safe for me to give and receive love in a way that feels good to me.
* ❋ The way I give love is unique and special to me. It is a gift to others.
* ❋ I am love.
* ❋ I release anywhere I've believed, or let others convince me, that I am not worthy of love.
* ❋ I release any expectations, projections, or conditions, from myself or others, of how love looks or feels.

Additional Thoughts

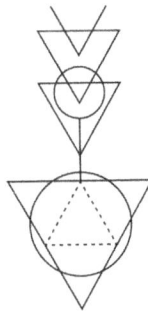

Day 11

No Purchase Necessary

"Everything in nature invites us constantly to be what we are."
~ Gretel Ehrlich

Since the beginning of human history we have appreciated the magic of nature. Explorers looked to nature for guidance and answers, and we still turn to it every day for solutions—be it food, medicine, dyes for clothes or decorations, and shelter.

We also know that bodies and their systems can sync with the cycles and rhythms of the oceans and the moon. A simple internet search will bring up tons of research about the positive effects of spending time outdoors and how fresh air and sunlight are so beneficial. Even concepts like grounding and using the Earth's charge to rebalance the harmony in our bodies are a thing! Like many children, growing up I spent lots of time outdoors. I wasn't aware of the benefits—I just loved it. As an adult, I've had to find ways to intentionally get outside and enjoy nature.

Through the years, I've discovered that being in nature is much more than just sunbathing and getting fresh air. Increasing your calm by listening to ocean waves crash against the shore is one thing; using nature for medicine and healing…well, that's a whole other ballgame! That's where we're going today because I'm here to tell you I've directly experienced the benefits of that and I shout my gratitude from the rooftops every chance I get.

The first experience that opened my mind to the possibility of using nature as medicine was with essential oils. After my first Reiki training, I got really sick because my body wanted to purge a lot in a short time. For two weeks I had "bronchitis-like" symptoms that the antibiotics prescribed by urgent care would not fix. I was miserable, not sleeping or eating and unable to work. Finally, I mentioned something to my teacher and she gave me a few oils, rubbed some on me, and gave some instructions. Three days later I had improved and less than a week later I was completely fine. I had never experienced anything like that before, I knew something magical had occurred.

Has something like that ever happened to you? Where you took a leap of faith, tried something different, and a miracle happened? Just think about it, I'll bet you can come up with one example.

Since then, I've dedicated lots of time and energy to learn about oils, plant medicine, and other natural solutions to help myself and others. I had no idea there was so much to know! How could I have missed out on this for so long?! After this experience, I started incorporating oils into my daily life and started to have even more benefits for my body. This made me think, *What else can I do to add more natural things to my day?* Thus, the research and inquiry began. The more I learned, the more I started to add and remove things from my diet. My body started responding in a good way and I was amazed by how easy some of it was to do. Yes, it was more involved than eating more fruits and veggies, but it was completely manageable.

To this day, I seek to improve my understanding of how nature can help us heal our bodies and increase their flow—from diet to simply being in nature and allowing ourselves to connect with the trees, flowers, birds, and other elements. There's such a natural rhythm and ease when you sit and observe nature; for example, the natural cycles of destruction and creation that we'll talk about on Day 19 and the ease with which they occur—the perfection in leaf shapes and flower construction. I'm extremely grateful for the information I've gained over the years to help myself and my clients benefit from nature's healing powers each day. So, we give big gratitude for nature and all of the magic made possible because of it.

Today's Exploration

Exercise

Today's exercise is very easy. Go for a walk and spend intentional time in nature. Hear the birds, admire the trees and flowers, touch the grass, and feel the natural rhythms. When you do this, see how your body feels and if you notice any difference. Then report back. That's it!

Questions

1. How did your body feel?

_____

_____

_____

2. What did you notice that you wouldn't normally see or hear?

_____

_____

_____

3. Did you have any new awareness or information come in?

_____

_____

_____

4. Did you notice any changes in your body or mood after your time outside?

_____

_____

_____

Daily Clearing

- ❋ I am at one with nature and in flow with Her rhythms, which provide guidance for me and my body.
- ❋ I release anywhere I've disconnected myself, or allowed others to disconnect me, from nature and the wisdom it has.
- ❋ I give myself permission to receive all of the goodness nature has to offer and to be in flow with that.
- ❋ I am open to receive any and all healing nature wants to provide to me.
- ❋ I am grateful for all of the gifts nature provides and the ability of myself and my body to benefit from them.

Additional Thoughts

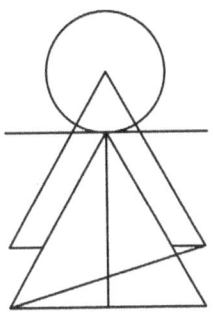

Day 12

Shout-out to My Tribe

*"At times our own light goes out and is rekindled by a spark from another person.
Each of us has cause to think with deep gratitude of those
who have lighted the flame within us."*
~ Albert Schweitzer

Friendship is an interesting thing because over time we have different types of friends and they serve different purposes in our lives, just as we serve different purposes in theirs. Friends evolve as we and needs do. It is indeed an evolution because some have friend groups that last decades, while others are dependent upon hobbies, jobs, children, or pets. None of these situations are right or wrong, they simply contribute to the variety in our life experience. That is what we're celebrating today.

When I was in consulting we used a tool to manage our networks and all the people in them. Think of concentric circles. Each circle represented a category of people.

- Strategic: The people who could help you find opportunities, provide career guidance, and have your back when navigating politics.
- Peers: The people you called to have an honest conversation with because you need help with a template, brainstorming, you were asked to do something on a ridiculous deadline, or just needed a shoulder to cry on.

- Assistance: These were the people who were a level below you and you could offer them an opportunity to help you.

Many people I worked with used a tool like this, and I find that I'm applying it now to friends and others in my personal life. There are still circles, but the people don't fit as squarely in one or the other. They also appear and reappear as time passes. As little kids, we have friends to play with, go to sleepovers and birthday parties with, and maybe even study or play sports with. That changes as we weave in and out of the concentric circles for a variety of reasons. We switch jobs, move to different cities, raise families, and have pets. All sorts of things change and our circles change with them. The consistency fades.

Over time, my friends and community have shifted significantly, as has the nature of our relationships, the types of things we share with each other, and the things we need each other for. It's all evolved. But somehow, everyone has been there for a purpose, whether I've known it or not. Have you noticed that as the tides change, we always end up with the right people? It may not always seem like it when we're in the thick of it, but upon reflection, it all worked out somehow.

I don't know about you, but I have had a lot of change—and numerous shifts—over the last five years. One thing I had really wanted for a long time was community and strong friendships—people who I could trust and rely on for the good, bad, and ugly. I didn't have this the way I wanted, which makes me appreciate my community even more now. The types of people I needed have changed and the types of people who need me have changed too. Again, when I look back and see that despite all the changes in my life—and the people shifting in and out of the concentric circles—it has always been what it needed to be.

Have you had a situation where someone seems to disappear from your life, like water evaporating? It can be devastating, huh? When this happened to me I sometimes felt sad and other times I was happy—either way, I now know it was what was needed to support the shift. The people and energy needed to shift. The relationship had served its purpose. Thanks to the internet and social media we're able to stay in touch with people differently than we were years ago, but the relationships still change. I continue to be grateful for the people that I have in those concentric circles, as well as wherever I fit into theirs, because they never seem to fail.

The range of friendships is as varied as the colors of the rainbow, giving us the opportunity to share, love, see, and be seen in so many different ways. And because of this beautiful spectrum, the more people show up for me, the more I know how I want to show up for others, and the more I'm able to find other people like that. As our energy, goals, and needs shift, so do the things we need as support.

It can be a really beautiful experience when you connect with someone on an intimate level, in an emotionally safe and supportive way. You can let your guard down; you can shed all of the masks you think you have to wear. You don't have to compartmentalize yourself. You can call each other out when you're not stepping up or even being jerks. You can celebrate with each other as well. You can see and be seen. Do you have someone like that in your life? It's pretty special, isn't it? That's what we're celebrating today—friendship, connection, and community—so we can see the value they bring to our lives and what we bring to theirs.

Today's Exploration

Exercise

Today's exercise is very simple. We are contacting our community to let them know they mean something to us and we are grateful for them. That's it! Write 10 names in the spaces below (you can do more if you'd like) and contact them today using the method that feels best to you.

1. _____
2. _____
3. _____
4. _____
5. _____
6. _____
7. _____
8. _____
9. _____
10. _____

Daily Clearing

❋ I am grateful for the love and support I receive daily from those around me.

❋ I release everywhere I've decided I'm not allowed to have the community I desire/deserve.

❋ I receive all of the love and support my community wants to give me.

❋ I easily attract all of the friends, community, support, and partnerships I need.

❋ I am safe in all of my relationships and am valued for being me.

Additional Thoughts

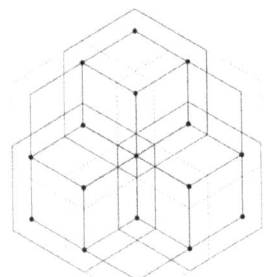

Day 13

Emotions (are Not the Enemy)

"To live without feeling is to watch without seeing."
~ K. Tolnoe

For most of my life, I didn't have a healthy relationship with emotions. Forgive me for the generalization, but I've found that most of us don't—probably because we are not taught to see, experience, or process our emotions. We don't allow ourselves to express them because of judgment or we simply do not know how. We question whether the timing is appropriate and fear the reactions of others when our emotions come up. Because of this we suppress them and don't take any action, which causes more harm.

It's taken many years to get to a point where I don't wear my emotions as I would a t-shirt. What I mean by that is the ability to say, "You know what? I'm experiencing this emotion but that is all," and then ask questions about what the emotion is trying to show me and take steps to work through it.

One question is, "What is the emotion in the first place?" That was a hard one for me because when I began this journey I used to joke about my emotional vocabulary. I think I could accurately name about five emotions: happy, sad, mad, frustrated, and confused, because I was not in touch with my emotions at all. I couldn't identify them and definitely didn't have healthy ways of processing them, so I suppressed, ignored, and just "let it be" for most of my life.

Can you identify with this?

My emotional band-aid was ripped off in 2016, during a visit home to Southern California. I had recently heard of this thing called Reiki and, after some research, was curious enough to book a session during that trip. Shortly thereafter, I found myself laying on a table, completely underwhelmed, as the practitioner told me my chakras were blocked. They said a few other things and sent me on my way. A few days later I started crying out of nowhere. No trigger, just ugly crying.

You know the ugly cry, don't you?

I remember feeling like I was crazy and out of control because all I wanted to do was cry. It felt like the right thing to do but I wasn't a "crier" so it scared me. This was one of the first times I allowed myself to follow what felt right, despite how "off" it seemed. Come to find out that was the beginning of the emotional journey. Decades of pent-up emotions were coming out—sometimes at the most inconvenient times. It was like a bad game of hide and seek. Ready or not, here I come! From there, I gained tools and resources to face my emotions head-on, learning to embrace rather than fear them. It started to feel good.

I was the strong one who always had it together. The stoic one who didn't usually express what I was feeling. That caused some difficulties, but having the right words to express has always been important to me, and given my limited emotional vocabulary it made more sense to stay quiet. My point is, I understand what it feels like when you may be feeling shame or guilt for not having the words to accurately or adequately express how you feel. The good news is there are tools and resources for us to use so we don't have to feel this way anymore.

Over the past five or six years I have also come to realize that we "carry" things (e.g. thoughts, beliefs, and emotions) for other people. We also process for others whether we want to or not. Our bodies let us know, but often we don't know that the body is actually talking to us. We don't know that we can have a relationship with our body, talk to and listen to it, and get to the core of why an emotion is coming up—or even why someone else is reacting to us in a certain way.

These awarenesses are part of how I operate now because I understand that my body, everything, is reacting to something else. Knowing the trigger and then being able to work through to the core of the issue of what's causing the feeling/emotion is powerful. We give ourselves the space to acknowledge the emotion and work through it, ignoring the ideals or roles we think we are supposed to play (e.g., males are macho and don't emote, or women are weak when emotional, or I can't express myself because of my environment). When we give ourselves permission to acknowledge, feel, and process we unlock a powerful force within us and invite the same for others. You have the power to choose whether and how you deal with your emotions and how they affect your day.

What would the world be like if we took two minutes to be accountable for our emotions and ask questions?

- I'm feeling a certain way, what is this about?
- What is the emotion that I'm experiencing?
- I wasn't feeling this way two hours ago—what happened to make me feel like this?
- Is there something I can learn from this?
- What can I do about it?

I've found that when I don't give myself permission to do this type of work, I may overlook something. When we take the time to dig a little, that's where the magic is.

There's so much to be grateful for when it comes to emotions—not just because they help us understand, but also because there are tools! I'm personally grateful for tools because for so many years I made myself wrong (and others did too) for not having the right words to express myself and/or knowing how or when to. I carried a lot of fear, guilt, shame, and anxiety around this—to a debilitating degree. Being afraid to feel and afraid to express is quite a dangerous combination! And I know I'm not alone because I've worked with many people who have experienced the same. Can you relate?

And what happens when we give ourselves permission to feel? I've been known to give some interesting homework to my clients, but this one is my favorite. I worked with a client who was uncomfortable expressing emotions, particularly anger. At the end of the session, I said, "You're going to think I'm crazy, but I want you to find someplace where you feel comfortable to let out a belly yell. Just yell and scream as long as you feel like your throat can handle it. Your body wants to release and this is a great way to do it." She looked at me a little surprised but said, "Okay, I'll try it." A couple of weeks later she sent me an email saying, "I did it! I screamed! When my family wasn't home I got in the shower and just let it rip. It felt amazing!" We have to give ourselves permission to do stuff like that instead of saying, "No, I don't get angry" or "I don't get sad" or whatever the thing is. Processing through these things is important, and when we don't give ourselves permission to do so we pay a price.

Today I am grateful for emotions, questions, and tools. Emotions help us remember we're alive because we're feeling. Questions help us understand what emotions we're feeling and why. Tools help us process the emotions so we can grow and move forward. It's a beautiful thing when we allow ourselves to experience the full spectrum and witness the same for others. Now, how about we dig in for you?

Today's Exploration

Questions

1. What is your relationship with your emotions?

_____

_____

_____

_____

2. Where did your relationship with emotions come from?

_____

_____

_____

_____

3. Have you experienced any impacts on your life or body because of your relationship with emotions?

_____

_____

_____

_____

4. Do you have examples of people who have good relationships with their emotions? Are you that example for others?

_____

_____

_____

_____

5. Can you think of any emotions that you are ready to release now? List them. You can look up emotion wheels to help identify what you're feeling.

_____

_____

_____

_____

6. If you can't accurately label the emotions you're feeling, what action can you take to release them anyway? Today, your mission is to release by any means necessary. If it's going for a walk, beating up a pillow, drawing, screaming in the shower, or having your own private dance party, I want you to give yourself and your body permission to release whatever is ready to go.

_____

_____

_____

_____

7. What action did you choose to release your emotions?

_____

_____

_____

_____

8. What did you feel in the process and how do you feel now that you're done?

_____

_____

_____

_____

Daily Clearing

❊ It is safe for me to experience and process my emotions.

❊ Anywhere my body is holding onto emotions that are ready to go, I give my body permission to release them now.

❊ I release any judgment I may be carrying from someone else who did not like the way I process or express my emotions.

❊ I release any judgment I may be carrying from myself for not having the words to accurately express how I feel.

❊ I love knowing that my emotions are guides and I can use them to support me.

Additional Thoughts

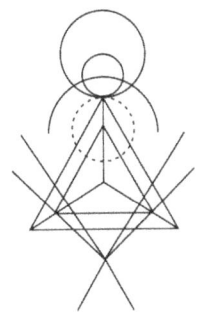

Day 14

See You, See Me

"No act of kindness, no matter how small, is ever wasted."
~ Aesop

Let's walk through a few scenarios to begin today. As we do, I'd like you to reflect on whether you've done any or all of them before. Have you ever:

- Criticized yourself for being tired and not being able to perform the way you wanted?
- Attended an event out of obligation, despite being exhausted, and as a result couldn't be your best?
- Knocked your presentation out of the park, but stayed up all night to prepare because that was the only time you had?
- Felt unwell and, despite your best efforts to force yourself, didn't do something/ go somewhere, then riddled yourself with guilt and shame as a result?

We're often not taught to take breaks or rest; instead, we're shown a model of working hard, long hours and striving for constant perfection. We're told that success, beauty, love, and health have to look a certain way. That productivity is more important than presence.

This was me for most of my life: an overachiever who defined success by accolades and sources outside of myself. External validation mattered to me so I pushed until I couldn't push anymore. I developed a reputation as someone who makes things happen, gets answers, and is responsible and reliable. I did many things out of obligation and pushed past my limits. I also made myself wrong if I couldn't give 100% or more all the time. I was full of judgment, blame, guilt, and shame if I couldn't get something done. If I couldn't stick to my word and give the world to someone (usually by sacrificing myself), I was somehow wrong. We all have deadlines and obligations, but what is the cost to complete them? We don't always know the price or how it will show up, but we pay.

Five years ago I wasn't able to prioritize my tasks based on what was best for me and stick to that (e.g. by picking the one or two things that absolutely needed to get done in a day and push the rest to tomorrow or another day). I didn't give myself a chance to relax or be flexible in my schedule. I never said, "This is where I am and that's got to be okay. So what can I do from here?"

How do we do this? We start by giving ourselves permission to feel things out, understand them, and ask questions without criticizing. When we ask questions, we get to dig around, gain clarity about what's going on, and uncover the steps needed to feel better. We get to take control of the narrative and choose how we treat ourselves and others—we can assess whether compassion is part of the picture.

I believe that one of the biggest lessons I was meant to experience from the diagnosis was to slow down and listen to my body. To give myself the grace and space to not be 100% all of the time. To not hold it together and give the impression that I have all the answers. It was to show compassion to myself and my experience—which some days entailed struggling to get out of the front door, perform at a job without giving any indication of discomfort/weakness, and returning home utterly depleted. And, through this, it was to understand how much compassion I can give to others for what they may be going through.

We all have something that we're dealing with, but how often do we simply allow that to be okay? To show up to the best of our ability and simply let that be okay? What if 60% is all you have to give today? Is that okay if you give your best? What about 40%? Are you any less worthy of being treated well, of being loved and respected, if that's all you have to give? This is a perspective shift I needed to make for myself because if I gave anything less than 90% there was something wrong with me. No one told me that; it was a self-imposed limitation.

One of several things I've changed in this learning is to be easier with myself and allow wherever I am to be perfect. Understanding that I have boundaries—physically, mentally, emotionally—and knowing that when I hit those limits I have a choice. I can go or stop, but I also give myself permission to step back, assess how I'm feeling, and decide how to proceed. I also let others react to my decision the way they'd like to. If I know that I've made the decision that is best for me, then give compassion, understanding, and grace to myself, that's all I can do. In the process, I am also inviting others to do the same.

Today, we celebrate grace and the ability to have, experience, and understand it. We celebrate compassion and where we give it to ourselves and others. Where we have allowed ourselves to receive it and be it. We are exploring ways to give ourselves compassion today, for everything that is and is not, in our lives. We are giving ourselves permission to deprogram everywhere we've prevented ourselves from the ease of this new journey.

Today's Exploration

Questions

1. Do you believe you show yourself the grace and compassion that you deserve? Why or why not?

_____

_____

_____

_____

2. Do you show others grace and compassion? How do you do this?

_____

_____

_____

_____

3. When was the last time you gave yourself permission to show grace and compassion to self? What was the circumstance? How did it feel?

_____

_____

_____

_____

4. What about when someone showed it to you?

_____

_____

_____

_____

5. Where does this behavior come from?

_____

_____

_____

_____

6. When you think about increasing grace and compassion in your life, what thoughts and feelings come up? Is this an area that is new or familiar to you?

_____

_____

_____

_____

7. What is an area in which you can show yourself a little more grace and compassion today?

_____

_____

_____

_____

8. What about others in your life?

_____

_____

_____

_____

Daily Clearing

* ❋ I forgive myself for all of the times when I didn't show myself the grace and compassion I deserved.
* ❋ I forgive others for not extending grace and compassion to me when I needed it, even if I couldn't see it myself.
* ❋ I am open to receiving all of the grace and compassion I deserve in my life.
* ❋ I release any and all blocks present in my life that are preventing me from seeing and experiencing the full experience of grace and compassion.
* ❋ It is easy for me to extend grace and compassion to myself and others.

Additional Thoughts

Day 15

Signs, Signs Everywhere

"I am open to synchronicities and do not allow expectations to hinder my path."
~ Dalai Lama

We've all had those signs—the repeating numbers, the call from a random person, an animal that keeps popping up. Do these things mean anything? Do we even think to ask? Furthermore, do we appreciate them and how powerful they can be? How many times do we have signs throughout the day and completely disregard them? We have all disregarded them at one point or another. We get busy with our daily lives and anything outside that routine goes unnoticed. I've found this to be the case when it comes to things like following our heart or intuition. We shut it down and it can be hard to train ourselves to turn it back on. But that's okay because there is a way to do just that!

I want to share two very different instances when I received signs. One morning I went to exercise—dancing—and decided to wear a pair of shoes I hadn't worn in a long time. I wanted to try them because they used to be really comfortable and had made it through the latest purge for donation. When I started dancing I noticed something on the floor, white sticky stuff. Then I noticed I was hearing a different sound on the floor and when I looked I saw it was a piece of the shoe coming off! The shoe glue wasn't sticky anymore and was barely holding things together. That's how long I had owned the shoes—many years. *Okay*, I thought to myself, *this is bad. My shoes are falling apart and I could hurt myself. I don't need to look fashionable exercising at home, but still, this is bad.* As I looked at the sticky white stuff on the floor, I started wondering about other things I may be holding onto that I no longer needed. I'd insisted on keeping the shoes because they looked good and at one point were very supportive, but that time had passed.

The second example was on my birthday and is a bit more dramatic. My plan was to go out dancing, and in preparation for the late night I decided to take a nap. When my alarm went off I found the excitement had waned and I no longer felt like going, but I was determined to go despite this feeling. As I got ready I changed my outfit more than normal, which was the second sign: indecision. From there, everything happened so fast. I was so focused on leaving that I didn't check my usual places to keep things; I just rushed out the door, letting it slam shut (and automatically lock) behind me. That's when I realized I had everything but my keys. I don't know if you do this, but I put my keys in the same spot so I don't forget them. When rushing, it makes life easier, but for some reason I didn't do it that day. There wasn't a master key for the building and the front desk had just closed, so I called a locksmith. I waited two hours for someone to come (they arrived at three a.m.) and they charged me two hundred dollars to unlock my door (in under a minute). That's how I spent my birthday evening…not dancing my heart out on the dance floor. I was so disappointed, but, OMG, the signs! This time they were more internal feelings that I ignored. You could also call it intuition, but they were signs nonetheless and I ignored them all because my ego wanted something.

Those are two very different examples of how I've experienced signs and synchronicities. Sometimes we have a flair for the dramatic because that's what we need to pay attention to and get the message, but other times the sign is as subtle as a whisper. Many times what we experience is confirmation that we're on the right path. I don't know about you, but I find those comforting.

On the other hand, looking for answers and forcing your way into activities may not be necessary—or helpful. We've all desperately wanted something to happen and have interpreted a sign simply because we wanted to. I'm okay fessing up to this if you are. We're in this together, remember?

What if there is guidance at your fingertips that you haven't been able to see or hear? Don't worry—if it's really important the signs will get bigger and louder so you can notice them. But as the quote in the beginning states, expectations about how things occur can hinder the magic that wants to unfold. Increasing our awareness is what helps the magic flow. I've also gotten a lot of "stumble upons" in my journey that I didn't always interpret as signs, but they were, and each one helped me grow in new and unexpected ways. You know you're in the right place because you're stumbling upon things, you're following your nudges, you're following your breadcrumbs.

Our bodies also give us signs. When we are tired, hungry, or have pain, that is a sign. We don't always listen, but that is a sign. One morning I was scrolling through social media and saw three videos about ginger. Then I saw an email explaining the benefits of ginger in recipes. Then, later in the day, I saw something else about ginger. I thought, *My goodness, I guess I need to add ginger to my diet for a little while to see what's going on!* That's how it happens, but we have to be able and willing to put the pieces together. And yes, I did go to the store to buy ginger and felt better after a few days.

We also receive signs in our dreams. There are many opinions on how to interpret dreams, so that can be confusing sometimes. But at the end of the day, our dreams are filled with signs and symbols that can help us in our awake state.

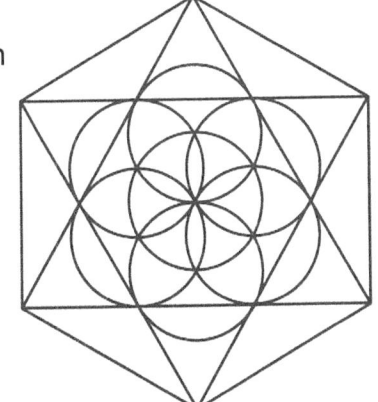

Here are some examples of signs:

- Seeing someone you hadn't seen in a while but were just thinking about
- Scrolling through your social media feed and seeing a picture or ad that supports a thought you've been thinking
- Seeing the same object across multiple platforms and aspects of your day
- Seeing repeating numbers on the clock or a license plate (or several plates) while driving

These are just a few of the signs we receive. For me, it hasn't always been easy to recognize the signs and then act on them. However, over time, I've learned that the more I pay attention to the little ones, the more big ones come. Again, it's like little breadcrumbs showing the way. Ultimately, I get to that pinnacle or something even better. You can do the same, just follow the breadcrumbs.

My shoes falling apart was a good reminder of the signs that I receive daily and a reminder to pay attention rather than dismissing them as insignificant. Our willingness to take a minute to think, interpret, and potentially act can be life-changing. Now that I'm open to how these synchronicities happen and judge them less, I welcome them and what they have for me. You can easily do this too!

Today we're celebrating signs and synchronicities because they are reminders of so many things, two of which are that you're on the right path and you're not alone.

Today's Exploration

Questions

1. Are you able to identify the signs and synchronicities that happen in your life?

_____

_____

_____

_____

2. What are three examples of signs you've received and noticed recently?

_____

_____

_____

_____

3. Were you able to interpret these signs and/or take an action because of them?

_____

_____

_____

_____

4. How did it feel to act on the sign? Is that something you normally do?

_____

_____

_____

_____

5. If you noticed the sign but didn't take an action, what was the reason?

_____

_____

_____

_____

6. I'd like you to increase your awareness of the signs around you for the next twenty-four hours. What happens and what do you make of it?

_____

_____

_____

_____

Daily Clearing

* I receive and interpret all of the signs and messages I'm meant to have with ease.
* I release anywhere I have believed or been convinced that I'm not able to receive and interpret the guidance looking for me.
* I am fully connected to the Divine and the Divine in me.
* I accept my ability to be a clear channel for all messages and information looking for me.

Additional Thoughts

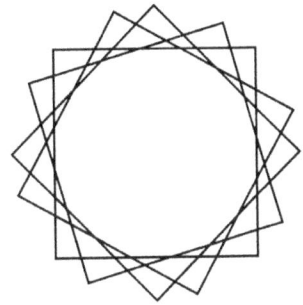

Day 16

Always Prepared

"Don't wait. The time will never be just right.
Start where you stand, and work whatever tools you may have at your command
and better tools will be found as you go along."
~ Napoleon Hill

When I got my first apartment one of the first things I did was buy a toolbox and fill it with some basic tools. I knew there would come a time when I'd need a hammer, screwdriver, or wrench so I wanted to be prepared. Thinking about how proactive I was with my bright orange toolbox and special left-handed hammer makes me wonder why we're not more diligent about acquiring tools to better manage our lives and ourselves. Furthermore, why are we not able to flex the tools that we do have as effectively when we need them?

We underestimate the value of our toolbox until we get in a sticky spot and need it. So today we celebrate all the tools we picked up along our journey to acknowledge them, but also to remind us that we have them if we need them.

Many Law of Attraction or metaphysical teachers will talk about energy and emotions. Emotions really are our primary guidance system. Prior to diving into this work, my vocabulary of emotions was extremely limited and my ability to process them was even less. It just wasn't my thing and I didn't know it was a problem until I did.

I used to have a pretty busy life and often felt stressed, overwhelmed, or lost. It's difficult to function when you feel like this, not to mention the potential health impacts that can happen. Many of us have obligations and responsibilities, leaving us with little time, know-how, or resources to quickly dissolve a feeling or situation. We know something is off or we're reacting or we don't feel good, but are not sure what to do about it. Or we have tools but don't always use them in the moment to feel better or get clarity. I know I wasn't taught that in school, so getting to a place where I started finding tools to help me communicate, deal with my emotions, and manage my stress was literally life-changing. And it was so comforting to know that I wasn't the only one who needed these things too!

Let's walk through a scenario with and without tools so you can see the difference. And don't worry—I identify with both so don't feel bad if you do too.

Scenario 1

You're in a conversation with a friend and you get upset. Something they said triggered an emotion in you. You don't understand why you are upset; you just are. Your friend notices your demeanor shift and asks what is wrong. You say, "Nothing," and shut down. You check out of the conversation and are mad at your friend, saying you need to leave. You are left with your emotions, unable to express how you're feeling, and a confused friend.

Scenario 2

You're in a conversation with a friend and you get upset. Something they said triggered an emotion in you. You don't understand why you are upset; you just are. Your friend notices your demeanor shift and asks what is wrong. You tell them you are upset and you don't understand why, then ask for a moment to understand your feelings and reaction. From there you start your inquiry: you said this, my reaction was that this is what I was thinking when I was listening to you, this is why I responded the way I did, and is this how I want to respond in this situation. Then you give yourself the grace to feel your feelings and your friend does the same. They even thank you for explaining the process because it helped them learn something.

What a difference, huh? Both of these have been me! Friend, Scenario 2 is a complete one-eighty from where I started. Have you ever had a moment like that? When you realize you used a tool, it worked, and you can give yourself a pat on the back because you see your growth? Please go ahead and pat yourself on the back now, because I know there is at least one time when you've done this.

It's also comforting to know that we don't have to go from complete fear and sadness to exaltation and full, unconditional love. We are human and are meant to experience the full spectrum of emotions, but I'm pretty sure you can't go from one side to the other with the snap of a finger or even the best tool. "So, Shannon," you might ask, "how do I get from this confused, weird state I'm in to the next rung up on the ladder? I don't even what know the next rung on the ladder is!" Well, you find something that feels good and go with it. Just one percent better than before and that's the next rung. It's that simple. And guess what? Your emotions and how you feel will tell you when you've gotten to the next rung and the next and so on.

Now I help other people do this in their lives—but that's after years of practicing with myself. I now have the vocabulary and the tools to use for and with myself to understand how I'm feeling when certain things come up. And it helps other people understand how I'm feeling and how I communicate but also can help them with their people as well. Everyone benefits!

Let me share some of my favorite tools with you and how I use them:

- *Asking questions.* I used to be afraid of asking questions, so this one is kind of ironic. But I love a good question! A good question can open up a new world and it can force you to consider things you never thought possible. This helps me more with emotions when I'm feeling triggered about something, or feeling stuck. Asking questions is an art form in and of itself, so it takes practice. But when you catch yourself in time to do it and not judge the answers, it's beautiful.

- *Journaling.* I've always been a writer so this is my go-to. It comes easily to me and has always helped me work out my thoughts, particularly when I didn't know how to make sense of them. I knew that I could express myself on paper without fearing judgment from someone else for not using the right words or trying to get them to understand. It was safe. Today, I write to gather my thoughts about a situation if I can't get a clear picture in my mind. It helps me feel calm and clear when I'm done.

- *Meditation.* Quieting the mind has been a more recent addition to my toolbox, and I've found tons of benefits from it. I started with guided meditations, but now I set a timer and sit in silence. I feel more clear and centered when I do it. I also feel more connected to my body and intuition throughout the day. When I feel like "I just can't deal" with what I'm doing in a given moment I'll stop and lay in the middle of the floor. Sounds a bit dramatic, but it really works to interrupt and refocus.

Like I said, these are just three of the tools I use regularly, so I'm just scratching the surface. But it is so nice to know that now I have a full toolbox, growing all the time, that can support my journey and I get to share my learning with others. It's time for you to do the same!

Today's Exploration

Exercise

Today we're taking an inventory of the tools you love, whether you use them for yourself or others. Pick the top five tools you use to maintain your sanity and get through the sticky spots in your life. In the table below, write out why they are amazing so you can remember why you love them and why they work.

What is the tool?	How did I get it? How do I use it?	Why do I love it?

Daily Clearing

* ❋   I have what I need to work through situations I experience in my life.
* ❋   I release everywhere I've decided or have been told that I don't have access to tools to better my life.
* ❋   I release anywhere I've blocked myself, or been blocked by someone else, from my natural ability to find/use tools.
* ❋   I am capable and confident in my ability to navigate through any situation I encounter.
* ❋   I'm grateful for all of the tools and resources I have access to, increasing the flow and ease in my life.

Additional Thoughts

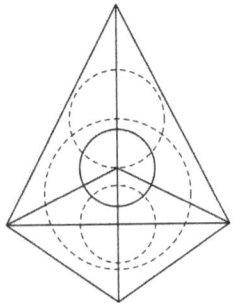

Day 17

Free Your Mind

"I never lose. I either win or learn."
~ Nelson Mandela

Years ago I stumbled upon the work of Abraham-Hicks, which was pivotal in my mindset journey. If you don't know their work, they teach the Law of Attraction, much like the book and movie of the same name, *The Secret.* I read *The Secret* in high school and thought the content was interesting, but it didn't resonate with me at the time. Several years later, Law of Attraction found me again right when I needed it. In my new, receptive state I remember thinking, *Okay, we can create things and we can create our reality. That's A LOT of responsibility!*

At the same time, I realized there was something very empowering about the ability to have a say in how my life goes. This new way of thinking was, well, *new* for me. It felt scary, but good. I liked the freedom of exploring new belief systems and asking questions so I could think differently—not in an academic way, but in an outside-the-box, challenging the norm of being stuck way. There's empowerment in realizing that there are things you can do in your life to be happy. And for the longest time, like many of us, I just wanted to be happy. I didn't know how it would happen, but I knew I would "know" happy when I found it.

It makes me think of first grade. We had a periodic segment dedicated to "critical thinking," with special workbooks to complete exercises. My friends and I would call this time "pitiful stinking" as a joke, but today I remember that and laugh because I love the ability to think critically and strategically about a topic and tackle it from multiple angles. This deep dive into Law of Attraction, mindset, and beliefs helped me rekindle that skill in a practical way. It's funny how little things like that stick with us, but become so integral to our lives.

Anyway, when I discovered this work, I was making several big decisions and trying to navigate them. There was a lot of doubt and imposter syndrome, and when it all came down to it, mindset was my biggest gap. I didn't know it either, which made it more fun. However, the process of learning was really rewarding because of the broad applicability of the teachings. And it wasn't only about thinking positive thoughts, it was training yourself to work through an issue or problem and have more confidence in your ability to navigate the situation; it was also about recovering if you needed to. For me, it was about moving from victim to victor by becoming an observer, asking questions, and learning more about people, in a way I hadn't known before. Who wouldn't find that valuable?!

I surrounded myself with this new way of thinking—at home, in the car, while commuting, every second I could—because it felt good. It let me know there was more out there for me and that I could access these things if I just believed it was possible. There are two statements that immediately stuck with me when I heard them and made me think. I refer to them constantly because of their applicability. Are you ready for them?

"You can't get it done. You can't get it wrong."

This one took time to sink in, but when I got it, I got it. As someone who was a perfectionist, I wanted perfection. I wanted it all and for it to be done right. I wanted to be first. If I wasn't the winner or at least second place, then something was wrong. I found ways to make things a competition. I had to be "successful" and I had to go the highest and achieve the most...just because. It was hardwired into me.

Needless to say, at first not being able to get it done and not being able to get it wrong was really frustrating. I wanted clear instructions that said, "This is where I'm going, this is what I'm going to do to get there, and when I'm there, I will know it." That's the "get it done" part. The "get it wrong" part was, well, what do you mean I can't get it wrong? There's a right and there's a wrong. You either get it done or you don't get it done. How is this possible?!

The lightbulb moment was understanding that the phrase means "you're always on the right path." This means you just have to take a step and learn whatever lesson you need to learn. Then you take the action, take the next step, learn the lesson, and repeat. You don't have to beat yourself up if you don't reach some ideal destination that probably doesn't exist in the first place. And that was a hard pill for me to swallow. Because, again, I was the overachiever who wanted a destination. And if I didn't, what was wrong with me? Can you feel me?!

Also, "I can't get it done" or "I can't get it wrong" requires a level of surrender, a level of flow, a level of taking the pressure off. I don't have to arrive at a certain place to justify my existence. I don't have to achieve a certain level to then demand a certain level of respect. There is no arrival. You just are. You just be. There's so much freedom in that because you take the pressure off yourself to constantly be on and just breathe. Go ahead and give a big exhale on that one.

That's not to say we shouldn't have goals and dreams. I absolutely have those and lots of plans to impact the world. What it's saying is that we can enjoy the process and give ourselves the grace and space for flexibility, and with less forcing. So, that's the first phrase that flipped my world upside down.

"*Everything is always working out for me.*"

Really? Are you sure, Shannon? Ha ha yes, just hear me out. This is really powerful because it invites you to take a step back and look at every situation, all of the components, and ask questions. I am a big fan of questions (remember pitiful stinking?).

When we're in the thick of a situation we don't always see everything, we just know we're feeling a certain way. Think about when you look at a map online. You enter an address and it takes you immediately to that address with little information about the surrounding area. But if you zoom out you're able to see the whole neighborhood. Zoom out some more and you see the whole town. That's what I'm referring to. When you're feeling all of the feelings, unable to see much outside of that, you're at the address. When you zoom out and see the neighborhood, you are in a space to ask questions because you have more information available to you. You can breathe and ask things like:

- What is actually going on here?
- If someone were thrown in the thick of it, what would they see?
- What are both sides?
- What is another perspective I can see?
- And then what am I missing?

Just because we don't think something is working out for us doesn't mean it isn't working in the grand scheme. If everything's always working out, then there's got to be a lesson, a silver lining, or some information I need to get my next step. There's got to be something to be grateful for.

Having this perspective of everything working out means there's no failure. I don't have to worry because I will get something from every experience as long as I allow myself to have that experience. I'll learn something in the process and maybe do something different later. If everything's always working out for me, then maybe now isn't the time and I am supposed to do something else first. The whole point of this is reducing worry, taking action, and having gratitude for what is before you. It is not about being high-vibe and happy all the time either, because that isn't realistic. We still feel the feelings, we just know there is something to be gained from the feelings and what it takes to process through them.

These two statements changed the game for me because they helped me see how limited my perspective was. Because of these statements, and other tools, I've been able to expand my perspective and learn to love questions. I've been able to dream bigger, believe in my capacity to achieve more, and take action. I no longer fall victim to circumstances (even though I do allow a periodic temper tantrum if it feels appropriate). I've also seen how my interactions with others have changed because of this new awareness. When we relate to others with a new mindset, entire relationships shift to ones where everyone learns and grows. And there's definitely something to be grateful for in that!

Today's Exploration

Exercise

Today we're looking at situations and asking questions. Below is a list of additional questions I like to use when I work through a tough spot. Think about the online map analogy I provided earlier and apply that to a situation you're going through in your life. It can be something current or something that may have been pulling your attention for a while, but the goal is to see a broader perspective and find gratitude in the experience.

What is the situation?

_____

_____

What's my view of what happened?

_____

_____

What feelings am I experiencing as a result?

_____

_____

If I zoomed out, what would I see?

_____

_____

If I saw from the other person's perspective, what would I see?

_____

_____

What is the lesson for me to experience?

_____

_____

If I zoom out again, what will I see?

_____

_____

What can I be grateful for in the experience?

_____

_____

Is there something I'm avoiding in the situation?

_____

_____

What can I see now that I'm able to look at it from more angles?

_____

_____

Daily Clearing

- ❋ Everything is always working out for me.
- ❋ I release everywhere I have ever believed that I'm not allowed to experience good in my life.
- ❋ I am always in the right place at the right time.
- ❋ I forgive myself for anywhere I've handed over control of my life and its outcomes.
- ❋ I am able to learn and grow from any situation I experience.
- ❋ I am constantly learning, growing, and improving myself.

Additional Thoughts

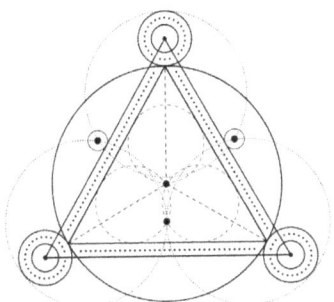

Day 18

My Body, The Temple

"The body says what words cannot."
~ Martha Graham

Did you know your body talks to you all day, each day? It also works in relation to your environment—a fact that is fundamentally misunderstood by a lot of people. I know a lot of us have a love-hate or even a hate-hate relationship with our bodies. I am grateful for my body, but that hasn't always been the case. This is where we are going today. We are looking at our relationship with our bodies and finding gratitude for them.

Actually, I should have said this first: our body simply wants to support us. That's all it knows to do. Just think of the acts of breathing, the heart pumping, and the blood circulating. We don't have to instruct the body to do these things; they just happen. Seriously, though, how stressful would it be if we had to tell our heart to pump or tell the blood where to go!? Thankfully, that's not the case. All the chemicals flow where needed and it all happens without having to ask. We are walking, talking miracles.

Now, sometimes those things don't happen in the way we would like them to. Again, this is because our body reacts to the things that are going on, both seen and unseen, in our environment. Studies and research have proven this. I think the body is a magnificent machine, the ultimate supercomputer. And for that reason, I have so much respect, love, compassion, understanding, and admiration for my body, what it goes through, and what it's capable of. The growth, strength, healing, and pure magic that is possible when we are in tune with our bodies is truly mind-blowing.

For a long time, I didn't have a relationship with my body and took it for granted. Growing up as a multi-sport athlete and dancer, I experienced several injuries, even concussions. You get hurt, take some pills, get back on the field. Or you go to physical therapy, rest, and return better than before. But you bounce back. What is interesting is I was always gentle with myself while injured or recovering. I had ankle surgery in middle school and was terrified of the pain. It was unbearable and I hated it. But once I recovered, I was back on the field and court, pushing myself harder than ever.

Then the years of pushing started to catch up; my body started experiencing some different things. Now, if you've ever had any kind of illness or diagnosis, you knew when something was happening. You may be in denial or you may go to the doctor, but you know. I was the "deal with it and figure it out because I'm strong and have it together" type of person (even though I was actually NOT together), so it took a while for me to go to the doctor. When I did, I received an autoimmune diagnosis and, eventually (after completely turning my life upside down to accommodate my body changes), was put on the right medication dosage. I found some semblance of normalcy...yet something still felt off.

I started looking for more answers on my own, and this ignited a spark like nothing   I'd felt before. I was on a mission. After five years of medication, another shift started to happen. My body started talking and I could hear it! The doctors had told me I'd be on medication for the rest of my life, but my body didn't accept that. I didn't have any proof that the messages my heart and intuition were giving me were possible, but

I had to trust them.

One thing led to another and more shifts happened. I rekindled friendships, entertained new ideas, met new people with new possibilities, and my world started to change. Remember when I told you about Reiki and emotions and crying out of nowhere? That was the beginning of my body's healing process. And the more I started to engage with energy healing, nutrition, alternative medicine, and plant-based medicine and oils, the more I realized how differently my body responded than it did to the pills and treatment I was doing. My body was leading me to an alternative pathway and I followed it.

After another year, my body said, "It's time for more change. I want something different. I no longer want medication. This is not for us. I know what the doctor said. I know what others say. I know the stories and beliefs and all these things that are ingrained into everything that everyone around you has told you, but I no longer want this." *Wow,* I thought. *I guess I have to figure something out to make this happen. I hear you, body.* Have you ever experienced anything like this, when you know in your heart something needs to change but it seems so outlandish that it's almost hard to believe? It feels scary, but right and good. That's what this was.

The next leg of the journey began, which was to figure out how to get to life after medication. I won't lie to you and say it was pretty, because it wasn't. But by way of strong community, thinking out of the box, creativity, and being willing to try anything, I was able to turn my life around again because I started building a relationship with my body. It took two years, but I was able to heed my body's request.

How many of us are unhappy with what our bodies are doing? How many of us are willing to do anything to make the situation change? How many of us say we're willing to do anything, but actually don't know what that means? Don't worry, this is not a place of judgment, simply one for questions and exploration. When it comes down to it, this journey can be downright hard, and when that rock bottom hits you have to know what you want and why. There's an element of trust and surrender that is required—and perseverance too. Our bodies fight for us every day and we get to choose whether we want to join the conversation.

Let's also talk about the shame and guilt that comes with our bodies. There are so many stigmas and ideals about beauty and what our bodies should be doing or how they should look. Mindset and beliefs absolutely tie into this because when we don't feel comfortable in our skin as a result of those pesky negative thoughts, our bodies hear us. I had lots of shame around what my body was doing, on top of other self-love issues, so I didn't tell anyone what I was going through. I was embarrassed and hid it as best I could. I made excuses about why I couldn't do certain activities because I was afraid of others' judgment. It wasn't until I started seeing how my mindset connected to this that I was able to make progress. My body was listening to my thoughts about myself and I was contributing to the problem.

I also had to be willing to get out of victimhood. Because I'll tell you, I didn't pitch a tent there—I built a house on a solid concrete foundation. I desperately wanted to know, Why me?! What had I done to deserve this? Who did I piss off to have my world flipped upside down? Today, I know that wasn't the case at all. It was about me finding my voice. It was about me developing a relationship with my body so I could guide others in their own process. It was about getting on my path of healer and catalyst, to uncover who I am, start to love myself, and build that self-worth, confidence, and compassion that we've been talking about in this book.

I now talk to my body all the time and thank it for supporting me. Thank you for getting me up the stairs, waking me up, allowing me to walk safely; thank you for digesting my food, and so on. I also express gratitude to make up for all those years when I didn't realize all it was doing for me, whether I was playing sports or at my lowest of lows, in tears with my face in the pillow, not wanting to do anything. I couldn't see that at the time, but my body was supporting me and, for that, I'm grateful. Whether we show up at 100%, or we're only able to show up at 50%, it's okay. If it's a couch day or a "kill it in the gym" day, just honor it, with no judgment. It's what the body needs to heal and go through whatever it's going through.

There has been so much learning and many connections through this process too. I wouldn't be able to approach working with my clients the way I do without this entire experience. I've always loved the body, but now I know why I had to understand how it works at a deeper level and the energetic impacts, and how all the layers need to be addressed in order to help it. It all makes sense!

Today I ask you, are you grateful for your body, even if it's just for getting up in the morning? Even if you're in pain or something happened and it doesn't feel 100%, can you still say you are grateful for your body? If you're on medication, dealing with a diagnosis, can you still say, "I am grateful?" And if not, what would it take to shift your perspective to say yes? What I will tell you is your body is supporting you and awaiting that conversation with you. It's whispering and giving you cues and supporting you.

Today's Exploration

Exercise

Today you are going to connect to your body and allow any and all emotions, thoughts, beliefs, and feelings to come up. I know it sounds a little heavy, but you'll feel better after. I'd like for you to sit with the statements below in the Daily Clearing section for 3-5 minutes each and write down everything that comes up without judgment—the first things that come up! There is no wrong way to do this so any information you get is perfect. Close your eyes, breathe deeply, receive the information, then write and repeat.

That's it! If the space provided isn't enough, feel free to grab your journal to keep going. You may also sit with the questions I posed above (at the end of the previous section) and write what comes up with those.

This is an exercise you can come back to any time you'd like because you'll find that your awareness about your body shifts each time and you're able to see more of the amazing magic your body works for you daily.

_____

_____

_____

_____

_____

_____

_____

_____

_____

_____

Daily Clearing

- ❋ I'm grateful to my body for supporting me each day without having to ask it.
- ❋ I release everywhere I've made my body wrong for not being something I thought it should be.
- ❋ Anywhere I'm feeling or have felt shame, resentment, or judgment against/ toward my body, I release it.
- ❋ I forgive myself for not knowing how to understand, work with, and love my body.
- ❋ Thank you, body!
- ❋ I'm grateful that my body knows exactly how to respond in every situation

and moment.

✳ It feels good to know that I am aligned—mind, body, and soul.

✳ I release anywhere I've believed that I can't be in sync with my body and understand what it does.

✳ I release anywhere I've blocked myself from having a relationship with my body because of expectations I've held.

Additional Thoughts

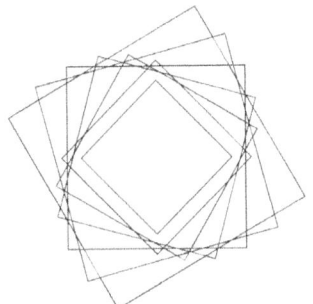

Day 19

Everything is Possible

*"When one door closes, another one opens;
but we often look so long and regrettably upon the closed door
that we do not see the one which has opened for us."
~ Alexander Graham Bell*

Has there ever been a period in your life when it seemed like there was constant change? Just one thing after the other, coming or going, and then…a period of stability. That's what we're talking about today—cycles of destruction and creation. And by destruction, I mean things changing and being removed. It seems like there have been several of these cycles in recent years, and it's interesting because in order for us to have newness and expansion, something needs to go. Something needs to disappear, or deliberately be burned down. And sometimes we're not willing to see that or even take the action to do the burning, to intentionally destroy.

I'm reminded of the Tower or Death cards in the tarot. Usually, when you get the Tower in a reading something's ending and it's up to you to perceive it as good or bad. But with every ending, there is a beginning. Whether we want it or not, the shifts will happen. Humpty Dumpty finds a way to get put back together again, right? So do we.

Let me share a destruction story I absolutely love because it is the one that made me really see the power of this work. More importantly, it made me see the value of these cycles. In my first consulting job, I was asked to work on-site at the client's office. This was new for me and I didn't know what to expect. Well, it ended up being difficult, but I tried my best because that's all I knew to do. One night I worked late and the client yelled at me. Completely shocked, I yelled right back. The next day I was asked to leave the project—and in a meeting with other people, no less! Shortly after that I left the company and found an amazing one that launched fourteen great years in consulting.

I look back on that situation and am grateful for it because I learned so much about myself, others, and office politics—so many lessons and growth that I pull from even today. There was destruction in leaving, but in the aftermath there was creation. And that's the juicy part because I got to ask questions like:

- Who do I want to be?
- How do I want to show up?
- Where do I want to work?
- What type of environment am I going to be comfortable working in?
- What type of people would I like to work around?

All from that experience! I can think of five other examples like this in my life when destruction happened and I had to pick up the pieces but ended up being better off afterward.

From an energetic and vibrational perspective this makes a lot of sense. One of my favorite illustrations of this is a scene from a book in James Redfield's *Celestine Prophecy* series. In it, the characters are vibrating at a higher frequency than the "bad guys" (and *maintain* the high vibration) and are able to elude them. I know that sounds "woo," but think about a time when you changed and then all of a sudden the people around you started to change. Or you worked at a job and because you learned new skills, you started to feel differently about your job. As you shift, so does your energy, and so does what you attract. This actually happens.

The first time this happened to me, I was very confused and upset. But eventually, I got to a point where I could see what happened and be grateful for that cycle running its course. Destruction is having certain relationships unfold in a way that you see they no longer are beneficial to you. They must drop off so you can keep moving toward your dreams and goals.

From an energetic standpoint, these people and situations are no longer matches and need to go. Also, things that are in that old vibration are not going to come near you, while things in the new vibration will! I had to learn that.

It was the destruction of certain relationships that caused this understanding. It wasn't quick or easy, but eventually, I could see how to use the experience as the launch point for my next phase. Destruction can be scary though, can't it? We can be afraid to let go because it's new territory and we don't know what it will look like. We stay in familiar waters because, well, it's what we know. They're comfortable and, while they could be better, they're not so bad. Have you rationalized in this way before? C'mon, I know I'm not the only one.

We've all been in circumstances that are uncomfortable and counter to our growth and health. In some instances, we have to choose whether to shift. You have to see that there's something not working, be willing to shed it, and then create from that new space. We have to leave a job, relationship, or town. Sometimes we have to let a belief go because it's no longer helping or keeps us in an old identity that isn't who we are anymore. Regardless of the situation, when we destroy, the clarity for creation comes. So, how do we get to the point where we can powerfully and intentionally choose to release what no longer serves us to create the life we want?

In quantum physics there is a concept called "zero point." It's where nothing exists but everything is possible. It's everything all at once. This happens in nature because there's always something dying, being born, or repurposed, particularly when there is a fire. I think of the maintenance fires I've seen in Africa. At certain times of the year you'll see huge fires set on purpose in open bushland to contain overgrowth. This is to create a more fertile, more fruitful environment for things to grow in the spring.

I'm grateful for destruction and creation because we learn so much in the process. We can't always see it, but we do, and we're able to shed things that no longer serve us so we can create from a more clear, stable, and expanded perspective. We're able to see what can come, what is meant to be, and even what we can dream. And when we do this for ourselves we're able to help others, which is where the real beauty lies.

Today's Exploration

Exercise

Have you ever set a maintenance fire, for your life? It's scary the first time you do it but feels good once it's done. You have clarity and space to create. Space to breathe and expand. What is in your life that has run its course but you may have been afraid to let it go? Or has something run its course and you're not ready to accept it yet? Either way, the cycle is happening. It's up to you how to deal with it.

Today, this is what we're looking at. You're going to look at where you can destroy something in your life, burn that maintenance fire so to speak, and what you can create now that there's space. We're looking at the process and seeing where there is room for gratitude.

Destruction

In the table below you have space to write down 3 areas in which to destroy. Take a few minutes to work through each area to get behind and understand why each area is something you want to address in your life. This is important before making any changes; we need to understand what it is and why it's been there for so long. If it feels relevant, ask your body and your intuition to help you clarify any changes and release what needs to take place for this to be as effective as possible.

What needs to go?	What benefit am I getting from holding on?	What is it costing me to keep?	What change am I ready to make?

Creation

Now that you've gotten some clarity around what can be burned down, it's time to create! In the table below you have space to write down 3 areas in which to create. Take a few minutes to work through each area to get behind and understand why each area is something you want to address in your life. Be as honest as you can with yourself. And don't worry, you don't need all the answers and steps, just some movement in the right direction.

What am I creating?	What benefit will I experience when I create this?	Do I have what I need to start?	What is my first step?

Daily Clearing

❋ It is safe for me to release things that no longer support me and my growth.

❋ I have the power to create anything I desire when I put my mind to it.

❋ The universe conspires for me to create the life I want.

❋ I love making space in my life for the things that matter to me.

❋ I love being in flow to know exactly when it is time to end and begin something.

❋ I feel empowered and in control of my life.

Additional Thoughts

Day 20

What Dreams Are Made Of

"All our dreams can come true, if we have the courage to pursue them."
~ Walt Disney

Remember when you were a child and you wanted to be forty-five different things when you grew up? Some even at the same time. A dentist who was also an astronaut. A circus performer who is also a professional racecar driver. Or even a dog trainer who is president and also a rocket scientist. Did you have aspirations like this, or was it just me?

We have our imaginary friends and make up all of these fun and seemingly outlandish stories about life and how it could be. But at some point we are told to get our head out of the clouds and stop dreaming. We're told to be "realistic" and that things like that don't happen—whatever "that" happens to be. We let the outside world, and others' perception of what is possible seep into our possibility and over time it slowly fades until it is gone.

Sometimes we're able to get this childlike imagination back and we're able to entertain it, while for others it is more difficult and may not come back.

But why is that? Are we afraid of what people will think if they knew our truest and deepest desires? Have we convinced ourselves that our dreams are so farfetched that they realistically can't come true? Or we personally don't see the path, or someone who has come close to the path, so we shut it down? I can identify with each of these questions and for a long time was afraid of what people would think if they knew my dreams. The fear of judgment is real, I know.

That's why today we are releasing all fears and letting our imagination run free! And you don't have to worry—it's between you and me, our little secret. Today we're showing gratitude for the dreams and desires that are there, that we can see or even just feel—be it owning a bike shop by the sea, running an animal sanctuary, or even starting a non-profit for troubled youth. Today is the day to let all of the dreams surface and give them some airspace.

Letting our imagination run free is good for us for several reasons. It gets us out of the day-to-day routine, flexes the muscles in different areas of the brain, opens us up to more intuitive information, and shifts our energy in a good way. Did you know that when you spend time in this space, daydreaming and releasing the need to know how it happens, the subconscious follows? Yup, it doesn't know the difference between the dream and reality, so if it's registering that you're feeling good thinking about the bike shop, it'll bring you more of that. Cool, huh?!

I know for me, getting caught up in how something will happen trips me up. I want to know when and how, so I'm prepared. Do you do that too? Well, that slows the process down. Our job is to dream, believe, and take action that feels good toward the dream. All of the pesky thoughts and beliefs, and others who talk about reality and limitations—they can be dealt with. But when you know something in your heart, you just know it and believe until you make it happen.

The dreams are there for a reason. What if there is a version of us out there somewhere that already has the thing you're dreaming of and is living that life? If something like that is true, then It's our future self calling us toward the things that light us up.

I've had several dreams for years that never seemed like they would come true. One of them is this book. Another dream was a health and wellness business. Over fifteen years this idea has gone through several iterations and countless attempts at making it happen. I can't tell you the number of times I've questioned whether it was going to happen and if all the ideas I had were valid or even possible. What I didn't know was certain experiences needed to happen so I could gain knowledge and shed layers of programming so I could receive the information to build the business the way it wanted to be built. I couldn't see the pieces or how they fit together, I just knew I was following a desire and breadcrumbs. Now I get to help people every day with their health and wellness and I love it! And nothing happened the way I thought it would. That's the funny, scary, and beautiful part of it.

We have to be willing to follow the breadcrumbs and our intuition and see where it leads us. What if we had the audacity to go after our dreams? What if we took the first step, big or small, and watched what happened? I'm grateful for these little thoughts and desires because they keep me engaged. They keep me curious about what else I can do with my life. Where else can I grow and be a better version of me? These are the questions you are going to think about today, in addition to giving yourself permission to intentionally put your head in the clouds.

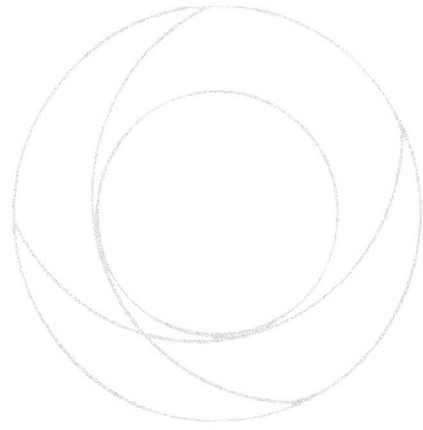

Exercise

List 10 dreams and aspirations you have just for yourself. Think big and let your imagination run wild.

1. _____
2. _____
3. _____
4. _____
5. _____
6. _____
7. _____
8. _____
9. _____
10. _____

Pick one and I want you to set a timer and visualize yourself achieving this desire. How does it feel? Who is there? What are you wearing? Fill in as many details as possible.

From here you will write down some immediate action steps to get you on your way.

Pick one that you can start working toward if you aren't already. Why is this the one you picked? What will you gain when you obtain it that you don't have now? What are 3 steps you can take in the next month to get started?

_____

_____

_____

_____

_____

Daily Clearing

* ❋   I release any judgments from others about my dreams.
* ❋   It is safe for me to dream and have big aspirations for myself.
* ❋   I release anywhere I've blocked my ability to let my imagination run free and dream with ease.
* ❋   I release the need to know how my dreams are going to come true and any expectations about how much dreams unfold.
* ❋   I trust I am supported and guided to all of the best steps to make my dreams happen.

Additional Thoughts

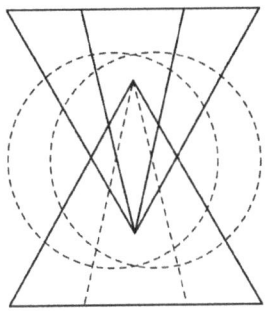

Day 21

Detours are Welcome

"Life is a journey, not a destination."
~ Ralph Waldo Emerson

Can you believe it?! You made it to the end of this journey! I'm so proud of you because you decided to commit to yourself, enhance your gratitude, and create a better life for yourself. Not everyone does that, so today we're celebrating this and your life journey.

When I started thinking about life as a journey instead of being focused on reaching destinations, I started to feel better. I learned that I can take the scenic route and that's okay because I'm still taking action. I'm probably going to learn some really cool things along the way, meet some interesting people, and grow beyond my imagination. I'll get where and what I need.

I sometimes joke and say there is an asterisk by my name because I have such a diverse background and set of interests. But you know what? Each piece I've gathered on my journey has been valuable to my puzzle and they all fit together to contribute to my experience. It's all been necessary and makes me ME. And that's what today is all about—celebrating your journey and seeing how it's made you YOU.

Have you been surrendering to your journey or trying to force activities, destinations, and outcomes? I used to be what I call a "master orchestrator," which means I felt I needed to control everything about a situation. I could make a plan for just about anything, so I did the research and figured out all of the steps, pros, cons, risks, and benefits. I spent lots of time focused on the details to make sure nothing went wrong. I had contingencies to the contingencies.

Sounds exhausting, huh? It was. When you spend time like that you aren't really living and enjoying anything because you're in a perpetual planning and re-planning cycle. I forced activities and was rarely in flow with my intuition. There would be an occasional, magical moment when I surrendered, but I needed control.

But what happens when we release the need to control and simply surrender to what is happening around you? Not in a way where we completely give up, but where we stop forcing our agendas, connect to our own energy, and flow. What I've found is the surrender doesn't always make sense. It seems sometimes like I'm moving backward or what I perceive to be out of order. But what also happens is I get so much out of the process because I learn about myself, clear layers, gain experience, and get more of what I need to achieve my goals. I get "there," wherever that may happen to be. Have you noticed the difference in forcing versus surrender too?

When we are willing to release the need to know all the details and invite our internal guidance to lead the way, life can be good. We can see and experience so much more than we thought possible. And we can see how much more we really are and what we're able to contribute. That's the journey.

Today's Exploration

Exercise

Today you are celebrating your journey. Although it isn't over, there is so much to be grateful for to this point. You are going to write a letter to yourself—but to the version of you one year from now. In your letter, you will say how grateful you are for everything that got you to today, your growth and new awareness, then for everything that is coming and developing on your journey. Indicate your excitement for what you're creating in your life and the fun you're having in the process. Make sure to put today's date on it, seal it in an envelope and store it in a safe place, and set a reminder to open it one year from now.

Daily Clearing

- ❋ I am grateful for all parts of my journey because they make me who I am.
- ❋ I release any judgment I've placed upon myself, or have adopted from others, about how my journey should look or feel.
- ❋ I am grateful for my ability to learn and grow on my journey, picking up all of the pieces I need to succeed in a way that feels good to me.
- ❋ I am grateful for the ability to change my perspective about my journey at any time.
- ❋ I release any expectations about how my journey should look, feel, or how I arrive.
- ❋ I forgive myself for anywhere I haven't been able to fully surrender to the fullest experience of my journey and invite all the expansion I am ready to receive!

Additional Thoughts

In Conclusion...

Thank you for coming along on this incredible 21-day journey with me. I hope you've had as much fun as I have. Some topics may have been a little heavy, but in the heavy, there is so much healing. Are you feeling any lighter? Can you see how much you have to be grateful for in your life? I trust that you do, and that perhaps you've even had some magical developments take place in this process.

Feel free to come back to the full challenge or any of the exercises any time you feel called to or need additional support with your gratitude practice. Gratitude, as you now know, is a mindset and way of life. It's something you live, eat, breathe, be. Switching to this perspective can take a little work, but it's easy once you get used to it. And it's one of the most rewarding things you can do for yourself. I'm wishing you nothing but the best as you continue on this gratitude journey.

Yours in gratitude,

Shannon

Shannon N. Smith

About the Author

Shannon N. Smith is a speaker, author, coach, and healer. She is the owner of SNS Wellness, a health and wellness company with a mission to educate, empower, and elevate individuals in their health, healing, and life journeys. A lifelong lover of the body, Shannon specializes in "whole body alignment" merging concepts from energy work and science to assist clients in reconnecting to their bodies and unlocking their own magic. Her clients feel a deeper sense of connection to their intuition and bodies to achieve their goals and live fuller lives. When she is not creating or serving others you can find her in one of her happy places...by the ocean or in the African bush.

Connect with Shannon:

Shannon N. Smith

CEO & Owner

SNS Wellness / Your Wellness Sanctuary

www.shannonnsmith.com

hello@shannonnsmith.com